'My life, when I think about it, seemed to begin with dogs. My childhood was full of them. There was grandfather's famous collie, Bess, who had a wild litter in a hole in a bank, and old Toss, who saved my life when I was about to drown in a waterlogged dung midden. There was old Jimmie Milligan's wonderful sheep dog, and Jack, the poacher's dog used for the long net and hunting the potato rows. There was Help who had a fight that started a family feud, and Jackie who mourned my grandfather's death . . . I never bought a dog but had them thrust upon me. I was never a "dog-lover". I have always had a great respect for dogs in their own right . . .' and in this book Ian Niall writes of the dogs in his life, their mannerisms, abilities and quirks of character. The most appealing portrait in this varied gallery is that of Susy who lived with the family for over fifteen years. When Ian Niall wrote her obituary in *Country Life* he received hundreds of letters from readers who felt they had come to know this little Cairn terrier personally.

Ian Niall

One Man and His Dogs

An account of a number of dogs I had in my life,
but one in particular – Susy, to whose memory
this book is dedicated

Futura Publications Limited
A Futura Book

A Futura Book

First published in Great Britain by
William Heinemann Limited in 1975
First Futura Publications edition 1978

ISBN 0 7088 1342 9
Printed by
William Collins Sons & Co. Ltd
Glasgow

Futura Publications Limited
110 Warner Road, Camberwell
London SE5

Ah! Faites mon Dieu si vous me donnez la grâce
De vous voir face à face aux jours d'éternité,
Faites qu'un pauvre chien contemple face à face
Celui qui fût son Dieu parmi l'humanité.

FRANCIS JAMMES

Contents

I

All my Dog Days

THE relationship between man and dog can often be as complex as that between man and woman. We have, own, or are owned by dogs for a great variety of reasons, not all of them exactly to our credit. We all want to be loved. We want to dominate or to matter to something. The lonely ones want to share their world with something and it is often an animal long conditioned to living with man. The reduced communication is accepted because there is nothing else for it. We all know the woman who lavishes love upon the dog as the child she never had, and those past middle age who replace the departed youngsters with a dog more obedient and amenable to discipline than any child ever was. There are awkward fellows who need companionship and something to talk to that will never turn the word or answer back, no matter how unreasonable the argument! The dog is all things to all men. Comedians have made a chestnut of the joke about the poor fellow, brow-beaten and abused by the bar bully, going outside to kick his tormentor's dog. The poor dog so often becomes the butt of man's frustration whether he, the dog or the man, is aware of it or not. Alongside the complications of the relationship there is often tragedy for a dog that suddenly becomes redundant. In Victorian times, when the family pet was treated as something that could be easily replaced and (especially at the time of the muzzling of dogs order) was often quickly disowned, the unfortunate dog would be popped into a sack, along with two or three housebricks, and consigned to the depths of the nearest canal without so much as a valedictory word. People have improved a little, a cynic might suggest. We don't throw unwanted dogs into the canal any more, but some of us throw them out onto the hard shoulder of the motorway. Dogs can find their way home, but not many can travel a hundred miles or survive the ordeal of being so violently thrown away. Dog-lovers will writhe and groan in agony at the very thought of such cruelty, but it takes place. Every day hundreds of dogs are turned loose, thrown away and rejected. Every day in some distant country if not in our own, someone dies of starvation. Their misery is ammunition for the politicians when they need to create a diversion. But it is a mad world in which a 'dog-lover' takes a poodle to a beauty parlour for a trim, a shampoo and perhaps a blue rinse, turning it into a buffoon, and paying as much for this treatment as would keep a human being for a week. We are all to an extent sentimentalists about dogs but there is also a touch of vanity and hypocrisy in the way we accept the flattery of foreigners when they say we are a nation of dog-lovers. We didn't choose to accept Napoleon's description of us when it didn't feed our ego, but over the dog we step from one side of the fence to the other. A man and his dog goes so well with home and castle. Nearly everyone in a lifetime owns a dog or comes to the point of owning one. Some of us, born into families where the dog belonged already, were conditioned to the dog and the family could never be complete without it.

My life, when I think about it, seemed to begin with dogs. My childhood was full of them. There was grandfather's famous collie, Bess, who had a wild litter in a hole in a bank, and old Toss, who saved my life when I was about to drown in a waterlogged dung midden. There was old Jimmie Milligan's wonderful sheep dog, and Jeck, the poacher's dog used for the long net and hunting the potato rows. There was Help who had a fight that started a family feud, and Jackie who mourned my grandfather's death. I recall so many, not the least of them Tweed, who met his end before the firing squad. I have hunted with dogs, fox terriers, a shaggy Welsh foxhound, my own gun-dog and not a few borrowed for the occasion when I went shooting. I never bought a dog but had them thrust upon me. I was never a 'dog-lover'. I have always had a great respect for dogs in their own right, not as pets or slaves, the lap dog or the peasant's overworked cur kept in an outhouse, but the animal that ran alongside man when he began to hunt and has thrown in his lot with him ever since, although accused of fawning on him. Man tends to regard himself as *the* superior animal. His creed tells him that he has an immortal soul. His priests have gone so far as to say that 'lesser animals' were put on earth for his enjoyment. A dog has no soul, they say. I suppose the dogmatists began to have some vision of a rather cluttered-up heaven should all man's pets be admitted to the holy place. There has often been talk of the hounds of hell, but never a word about a dog at the gate keeping St Peter company! Dogs at gates tend to misbehave themselves and would God be able to hear himself speak if dogs and their masters were reunited?

Three dogs in succession were wished upon me after I was married. I was fascinated by the first and pleased with the second. The third proved to be the dog of my life. If there are no dogs in heaven I don't care to go there. When Susy died I cried. I mourned her passing and the thought of it, long afterwards, brings me anguish, though she died at a dog's fourscore and ten. As they say about old people when they die, she had had a good life. She really had, and I was fortunate in living at the same time. I hasten to say that she was no showbench animal but the runt of a litter, a cairn with an undershot jaw. She took possession of me and changed my outlook entirely.

Susy's story is a good part of what follows because I knew her longer than any other dog—$15\frac{1}{2}$ years. I had made her famous through my weekly piece in *Country Life*. The thing grew week by week after I first mentioned her arrival in Wales from Wester Ross. This was a very long journey for a pup to make nailed up in a tea-chest and trundled from one junction to another—Oban to Perth and Perth to Glasgow, Glasgow to Carlisle, and Carlisle to Warrington (or was it Crewe?) and finally to Wales. When I first became a contributor to *Country Life* in 1950, I met Frank Whittaker who was its editor at that time. Whittaker was an unsentimental Yorkshireman and a journalist who had been through the mill. There was very little he didn't know about the craft. We were having lunch at his club and had retired to the lounge where gaitered bishops slept under newspapers and ancient waiters came and went. Whittaker lit his pipe as we sat down and said quite abruptly, 'What you need is a dog.' I concealed my surprise. He had perhaps, been summing up my qualifications as a journalist and considering the field I had chosen—country topics, natural history, fishing and shooting and the ragbag of folklore. 'Get a dog and write about it,' he went on. 'People love dogs and love to read about them. You will make friends through your dog and you will acquire a following. Think of Godfrey Winn. What did he have but a mother and a dog called Sponge?' This was a somewhat harsh assessment of Mr Winn who certainly had a great following at that time, not all of it attributable to a dog called Sponge. I hesitated to say that I had a mother and perhaps I could get by without a dog. Whittaker's sense of humour wasn't exactly elastic and I wasn't brave enough to oppose him. By the time he retired he knew I had taken his advice, or seemed to have taken it. I didn't bother to tell him I hadn't sought out the famous dog. She had come to me.

I can only say that Whittaker, who died some years ago, was right. He knew about dogs and people. At first I had felt that getting a dog and writing about her was admitting to myself that my imagination was limited to an extent that made me unfit to write a weekly piece. I had, however, had some experience in this kind of journalism. I had written a weekly column for *The Spectator* for seven years— without feeling the need for a dog! When all at once the dog was there and I mentioned her I was aware that I had created a character, to be compared with other dogs of the same breed and many who were not. When Susy displayed some quirk of behaviour I was told of similar quirks in other dogs. When she was off colour people offered medicine. When she was convalescing they sent her chocolate-coated raisins. I once remarked that she displayed a little stiffness after being out on a particularly wet day. Immediately there arrived through the post a full bottle of Carter's little liver pills which a kind lady felt sure would clear up the impurities in Susy's bloodstream, or urine, and banish all danger of the screws. I thanked the lady but withheld the cure for a few days to allow Susy to recover of her own accord. It turned out that I had to mention her at least once a month or letters would arrive enquiring about her health. When she was off colour there were get-well cards from dogs in America and South Africa as well as Britain. Christmas never passed without half a dozen cards addressed to Susy, signed on behalf of dogs in Cornwall and Wester Ross.

Did I say I was possessed? Having been brought up with and known a variety of dogs, lurcher, sheepdog, greyhound, spaniel, hound and terrier, I felt that I knew dogs. I had owned and trained a gundog. I knew that dogs were more than four legs and a tail with a body to keep these apart. Dogs are clever or stupid. I had had one that brought up my morning newspaper. I had known one that needed only a whispered word to get him to bring two hundred sheep to a fence to be counted. My grandfather had had one that brought him whisky from the inn and tobacco from the grocer's shop. My aunts had had a collie who would wail pitifully when they praised the cat. Susy came into our lives, took over the family, who surrendered without a struggle, and lived to make us part of her litter, dominating us in her old age as a very strong-willed old grandmother might have dominated us. We let this happen, even while we reserved a slight scorn for people who made idols of their pets! The truth was we were ripe for takeover. We were bewitched.

There are people who will put off a much-needed holiday for a dog's sake. There are some who turn down lucrative positions because the appointment might part them from a much loved pet. There are many people who 'waste' their substance tending old and infirm dogs, giving them the devotion others hardly give their aged relatives. People will leave hotels where their pets are not welcome and if this 'eccentric' behaviour is in the extreme, it balances the cruelty of those who regard animals as expendable or leave them locked up in sheds and caravans. Man has a great responsibility towards the creatures with whom he shares the earth, although he is often not even aware of the fact. Between the monster and the fool there are many people who walk the middle path with a dog at their heels, their lives enriched by giving the dog a dog's life. I am fond of dogs whether they fawn upon me or not. Most of them I find take to me. I have only once been bitten by a dog. The culprit was a shaggy-haired old English sheepdog who crept up behind me and bit me on the calf of the leg. I was still in short trousers, home on holiday from London. The owner of the dog was highly amused. 'Well,' he said, 'the English sheepdog isn't much of a dog anyway. A Scotch dog would have come at you from the front and had you down in a minute!' I have been wary of shaggy dogs ever since. No breed of dog is particularly treacherous or vicious. Dogs vary as much as their owners vary. Soft-hearted people have gentle dogs, staid and sober people seem to have glum dogs. Vicious people have vicious dogs and treacherous people treacherous dogs. Let me get to know a man's dog and I will tell you the nature of the man. Psychiatrists could do better if they studied the dog before leading their patient to the couch. I am quite convinced that man shapes the character of the dog and the dog reflects its treatment like a mirror. I have been regularly beaten, the sad eyes say. I am thrashed without mercy, the snarling dog says. I am mad as a hatter, fond of my belly and a place by the fire, insecure, neurotic. . . .

Gentle Susy was the idol of my family. In her case the dog improved the man. Nothing is completely one-sided. When she died I wrote her obituary for readers of *Country Life*. A great many people wrote to me at once. After the first hundred letters I had to give up my attempt to reply to them all. Among the messages was a verse by a French poet quoted by a lady who wrote to me from Switzerland. The verse is printed under the title of this book. As I choose to translate it and trusting that my French master doesn't turn in his grave, it runs, God, if you will grant me the grace to meet you face to face in the days of eternity, let a poor dog meet face to face he who was his god among men. Give or take a word or two it only matters that the poet conveys my own deep feeling about a dog. I was her God but the worship was mutual and Susy never lost her independence and dignity which made me love her more. The way she came to meet me, even when she was old and slow, the welcome she gave me, taught me something about the bigness of a dog's heart and its loyalty. There were times when she bestowed her affection on individual members of the family quite unaccountably. She would single out this particularly favoured one by burying a greasy bone under the counterpane of their bed. There was nothing more she could do to show her affection. She wasn't a mean or sulking dog, but gentle. By human standards she was mature. When I think about it, now that I have doubts about the hereafter and the existence of a soul beyond the death of the human body, I have had my share of heaven and hell. Hell was made more bearable and heaven more delightful by the fact that I shared $15\frac{1}{2}$ years with a small dog, a little runt of a cairn terrier called Susy who now lies buried a few yards from the door of my house.

2

Why I am Here

ALTHOUGH I can hardly remember the first dog I saw when I was a child of eighteen months it was almost certainly a collie bitch by the name of Bess. There were two dogs in my grandfather's house, an old one and a young one. This was generally the way. When it came to working dogs unless a young one was trained with an older one there would invariably be a period in which someone had to deputize for the dog and run after cattle or sheep. No one who hasn't lived in a farming community can really appreciate just how much a working dog does and how fearful is the burden when the dog falls sick and dies unless he has had an understudy. Toss was Bess's understudy in almost everything but there was one thing in which Toss could never be Bess's equal. Bess had come from the town to the farm. Grandfather before his removal to the farm had been a blacksmith. He had had smithies in several different places in his native county and while he operated what was to be his last smithy, grandmother applied herself to her trade of dairymaid. She was a very highly qualified cheesemaker and dairy manageress and not a mere milker of cows. To prepare for their final move grandmother kept cows on rented fields on the outskirts of the town and had a dairy where she made butter. A dog brought the cows from the meadow and grandmother

9

needed only to tell Bess the time for the dog to do her job.
Between whiles Bess would take herself off to the smithy
to keep her master company. She liked the warmth of the
place and she liked the comings and goings of farmers and
ploughmen with their horses. Grandfather had a liking for
tobacco and smoked two or three ounces of black twist
every week. Now and again he would treat himself to a
stone jar of whisky, the kind of bottle with a thong
at its neck, ideal for tying to a dog's collar. When grandfather wanted whisky he would tell Bess and she would
trot off up into the town and present herself at the bar of
the Galloway Arms. The innkeeper knew what was wanted
and tied the stone bottle round her neck. Bess would lose
no time trotting back. Even the most bold of the town
loungers who spent all of their days propping corners
wouldn't dare to intercept or try to rob the dog. This wasn't
entirely due to Bess's ability to take evasive action or the
sharpness of her fangs, for her jaws were free to let her
bite, but to a great extent to her master's reputation.
Grandfather was a man who would stand no nonsense. He
was tall and powerful and very hot-tempered. Bess always
came back with her 'message' intact.

There were two words that Bess knew well. One was
whisky and the other tobacco. She never made a mistake
and presented herself at the wrong place or brought back
the wrong thing. In the beginning she carried a 'line' in
her collar, a piece of paper that was a sort of IOU for
whisky or tobacco. Over the years this became unnecessary
and the goods were tied on without either a promise to pay
or a piece of paper stipulating what quantity of these sub-
stances was required. The town took a delight in watching
Bess do her work. When she had spent the afternoon at
the smithy grandfather would look at his watch and tell
her it was time to 'go home and help the mistress' and
Bess would trot off home to bring in the cows. When they
moved from the town, taking with them their livestock
and the ploughs and other tools grandfather had made

himself, Bess went too. She was after all, a very important member of the family. Toss was acquired to be her understudy. She might have remedied the matter herself in a year or two when she showed all the signs of having dallied with one of the dogs from a neighbouring farm and off she went to dig a great hole in the bank of a ditch and have a litter of pups like a wild dog or a wolf. The pups, I can faintly remember, were the wildest things anyone had ever encountered. Perhaps the warmth of the earthy cavern awakened the wild animal that was in them. They proved untameable. Bess came back to the kitchen. In due time her pups had to be destroyed before they could grow up to be sheep-worriers or something worse.

I can't remember Bess's end but I can remember the time when Toss was top dog. He was a shaggy, black and white Border collie with a broad head and a short muzzle. He was a serious sort of a dog, a working dog who did everything he was ordered to do without question. He was unusual in that he could work cattle and sheep. This is something a farmer hopes to find in a dog, but rarely does. A good sheep dog is trained from puppyhood to herd sheep the way they must be herded, by swift dashes, shadowing, a slinking, half crawl on the belly and a gentle ushering into fold or pen. The whole thing may be controlled by the whistle and everything is perfect when two or three dogs work as a team. Milking cows tend to react in panic if a dog runs quickly drops on its belly to watch them. They will lunge over a hedge or into a ditch and even hold back their milk if they are crowded into the byre or milking shed. Toss had undoubtedly begun his working life by being trained to sheep and had then been taught to jog gently along at the heels of a herd of cows, never going at a run but keeping the ladies on the move without frightening them. He had also been taught to turn a bull or separate him from his harem when he seemed determined to accompany them into the byre. Toss did all this. Sometimes when he was bored he would shepherd hens

from one place to another, making them cackle with indignation but when I arrived on the scene he had nothing
more to worry about. I was there to wander too close to the
great feet of the plough horses, to come face to face with
an old sow who wasn't at all inclined to give ground and
could bite a boy's leg off if she had a mind to. There was
the burn, carts coming in and out of the stackyard at hay-
time and corn harvest, and a procession of them to the
turnip house when the swedes were being lifted for winter
feed. Toss's job was to turn me as he turned the bull, keeping me out of danger and watching me with one eye while
he kept the other one open for a pig trying to slip under a
gate to go rooting in the corn or a cow heading for the
kitchen garden and the pea rows. One of the awful hazards
of the place was the midden across the road from the byre.
Every day the byre was swilled and scrubbed down with
endless tubs of water brought up from the pump or filled
at the burn. The water flowed to the midden making the
lower end of it an awful quagmire that lay hidden under a
crust that would barely support a lamb but allowed hens
and turkeys to cross with impunity. I was what they called
a 'stirring' child. I was never still and always on the brink
of some kind of disaster. Even with Toss as my shadow I
had managed to fall into the beery water of the burn when
it was brim full—and get out again like a half drowned rat.
One day when Toss was busy directing traffic or seeing
the loiterers down the road to the pasture I apparently
took it into my head to walk the midden's crust. It held
too, for several yards before, quite abruptly, I was swallowed up and sank until only my head remained above the
surface. Toss must have heard my frightened cry for he
arrived on the scene and began to bark. They were busy
milking. No one in those days had time to stand and stare.
Milkers milked and horsemen groomed their teams, the
dairymaid scalded cans and cooled the milk and a cat in
the hearth minded the porridge pot. It was hard to hear a
dog barking above the sound of spurting milk and the

clatter of churns. The ploughmen thought the dog barked the cattle to the field. Somehow Toss managed to make himself heard and all at once the folding door of the byre was thrown back and one of my aunts followed by my grandmother rushed out to discover what the alarm was about. Had I pulled over that boiling porridge pot or been attacked by old Sorbie, the sow? They could hear me calling faintly. They looked about and couldn't see me. I could see them, however, and I knew I was going deeper. 'I'm here, grannie!' I cried. Even opening my mouth would soon be impossible. 'Where are you son?' grandmother called in desperation. 'I'm down here in the dung,' I quavered and all at once they saw my head. Afterwards they said it might as easily have been a turnip on the midden. Risking being swallowed by the midden herself, grandmother rushed forward and grabbed me by the hair. A moment later she shifted her hold and had me by the head and I was hauled out just in time. Grandmother had to be swilled down with cold water from the pump. I was swilled down too and then wrapped up in an old blanket and nursed by the fire until a cauldron was boiled and I could be tubbed properly with a little carbolic in the water to freshen me up.

I am here because of Old Toss who not only saved me from the midden but turned an ugly Galloway bull when he seemed bent upon hammering me into the ground with that great lump of bone Galloways have instead of horns. I remember that day too, and another when Toss and grandfather faced the same bull when he had blood in his eye and refused to retreat. I learned something about the courage of men and dogs that day. Grandfather was lame and slow on his feet. He stood stock still and without a bullfighter's agility, kept the bull at bay with his walking stick. Toss was the cape, rushing forward, leaping sideways, darting back. The bull snorted and frothed but slowly he became mesmerized until he lifted his head and stared like a creature coming out of a fit and then he turned and ambled back the way he had come with Toss jog-trotting easily behind him, never for a moment letting out as much as a growl or a bark of triumph. He was a great dog although I think now that he had never known puppy-hood. I never knew him to play or run wild. He was old before his time, perhaps, and the weight of his responsi-bilities had made him so.

Before I was very much older Toss was pensioned and the dog that had been chosen as his understudy per-formed his daily tasks. The old dog still had his place of honour and took crusts from his master's knee when grandfather had his breakfast. He was one of the family and his happy retirement lay before him. He loved lying in the sun, on the flags of the steps leading down to the pump, on the crumbled dust of the old peat stack when the sun had warmed it and the hens had given up dust-bathing. Sometimes he lay on the dusty road itself. As time went on Toss's hearing began to fail, the way it fails old men. He could hear the high pitch of the grandfather clock's chimes but other sounds were lost upon him. If he didn't happen to feel the vibration of a milkcart coming up the road the man at the horse's head would have to stop and go for-ward and shake old Toss out of his dreams before the cart could pass. Toss surely herded sheep in the green pastures of his dreams and spent a long time doing it. One day the grocer came up the road in his van, making his weekly call to bring the few odd things not kept as stock in the larder. Toss didn't stir. The grocer must have thought him no more than a shadow on the road. All at once the van bumped as its wheels went over the old fellow and he was away for good to pen sheep in those Elysian folds he had only dreamed of before this day. The grocer climbed down and looked at him lying on the dusty road with blood coming from his ears and mouth. What could he say? He had killed a member of the family. Nothing he could say could make amends or bring the poor dog back. Everyone cried for poor Toss and remembered how he had saved me from the midden, turned the bull and scared away the would-be turkey thieves.

I remember him, more than fifty years afterwards, which may be remarkable to some people. I wonder about it myself when I am conscious of the fact that I have forgotten so many people who came into my life and went out of it. Some of those people went suddenly and tragically although not many of them did very much to make me remember them. Toss did save my life and I can see him now. I know the look on his face, the texture of those large dark eyes and the way his ears moved as he listened for the hurrying feet of the family coming back to the warmth of the kitchen on a winter's morning after the milk was away. He was no ordinary dog.

3

A Lurcher's Work

No dog is perfect, any more than man is perfect, and the fast dog almost always lacks the hunting cunning that would, to the poacher, make it perfect. The greyhound has speed but it isn't really the dog for a hare. The whippet too, is fast, but it lacks weight. The lurcher is the traditional poacher's dog. The gipsies and tinkers I saw as a boy all seemed to have a lurcher in tow, running at the back of the van or lying underneath it when they camped in some old quarry or on a bracken-grown verge. Crafty and cunning people have crafty and cunning dogs. Like the crow, the lurcher seems to know how society looks upon him. He is a thief and he is hardened to the world. He hardly needs to be sent in to steal a chicken but where the opportunity arises he will bring one back to his owner, perhaps because he might be reproved for not having done so. The very word lurcher means thief. Unlike the respectable man's dog, blundering into the farmyard, killing a chicken in his excitement, and causing a great outbreak of cackling in the process, the good lurcher works silently. Here one sees the collie ancestor coming out but then the collie is only a step away. The true lurcher is a first cross and not a mixed up mongrel whose inherited speed and intelligence may go out of balance as the blood mixes in later generations. I always wanted a lurcher but no one ever seemed to have one to give away. I knew all sorts of disreputable characters and they would have provided me with almost anything in the way of poaching equipment. A lurcher was something different, a dog that could always provide a man with his dinner and keep his family from starving. I didn't qualify among the have-nots. I was only on the fringe of the poaching fraternity. I should have to have bred my own. Lurchers aren't registered with the kennel club. They are as hard to come by as a good gun-dog, perhaps harder, and in the bad old days the very fact that a man had a lurcher at his heel told the world what his business was. A magistrate would prick up his ears when he heard the keeper say that he had taken so-and-so in such-and-such a wood with a stick in his hand and a lurcher at his heel. It was almost enough, in great-grand-father's time, to get a man transported to Australia.

If I never owned a poacher's dog I saw a lurcher work. It was owned by a man who worked for my grandfather occasionally. He wasn't what might be called casual labour, for he came when he felt he needed work and he was engaged when such help was needed. He was a notorious poacher. The keeper didn't approve of my grandfather harbouring such a man on his land, nor did a lot of his neighbours who let the rabbits at so much a season, for where he worked there would be snaring and trapping and long-netting, whether he had permission or not. Like the old fox, however, he left the area where he was holed up in peace and hardly ever broke the law there. Grandfather didn't let the rabbits but sometimes he gave someone the privilege of keeping them down. This was generally an old mole-trapper or a game-dealer, the former a one-legged man called Anton, and the latter the man who supplied us with fresh meat when we hadn't killed a lamb or a pig ourselves. The man with the lurcher lived about half a mile away in a 'cothouse'. The dog was never seen by day, but was there, all the same, sleeping in a shed at the back of the cottage while his master was at work. It was a 'dog for the dark' and it was well exercised from twilight onwards for his owner depended upon his snaring and netting activities to live without working for a good part of the year. The dog's name was Tam and he and his master were a perfect combination. The thing was in the blood of both of them, people said. The dog was bred from a fast greyhound and a very intelligent collie. His owner came of generations of poachers. The love of hunting, whether the hunting be legal or illegal, is a matter of heredity. A father initiates his sons, makes them his helpers, bloods them before they are past their formative years. These congenital poachers always knew every trick in the book and had an eye for the right kind of dog, knowing how to handle them. The basic difference between the lurcher and the ordinary gundog is in the way they operate. The gundog works in front of his master, quartering the ground inside a gunshot and maintaining that distance as they go forward from rushes to stubbles, from roots to thorns and thistles. The lurcher goes out and round and works back towards his owner. This brings whatever game they are after towards the snare, the net, the throwing stick or whatever weapon the poacher is using. The collie in the lurcher takes to this going out and coming round business naturally because a collie's main work is to herd in and round up animals rather than drive them off at speed. The collie too, will work quietly and with stealth that a gundog never needs to learn. The other half of the lurcher, the greyhound, lacks intelligence of the sort the collie possesses. It has been bred for speed and it moves after a hare with grace and beauty, overtaking it in a minute or two, so long as the hare doesn't begin jinking from one side to the other or losing himself in cover where the hare's speed means nothing and its sense of smell will prove inadequate. The hare's ways need to be anticipated and it takes a collie to work this out. Greyhounds chase hares but most of them are electric hares or stuffed specimens. The only time they see a living hare is when they are used for cours-

ing, a business that is little more than a tribal barbarity,
neither hunting nor sport, but something even the savages
gave up long ago. The speed of the greyhound and the
speed of the hare in action are not particularly well matched
and the greyhound will run over the hare and even tumble
on its own nose in the process, while the hare, recovering
in an instant, sets its ears flat on its rufous neck and makes
for the horizon. The beauty of it all would stop an ordinary
man in his tracks to admire the way a hare simply flows
over the undulating ground and the way a greyhound's
rhythmic movements carry it along. Put the collie with
the greyhound and something different happens. The
lurcher paces the hare. The hare jinks and the collie's intelligence takes over. The hare turns into the jaws of the
ferocious collie. The greyhound is too soft a creature to be
able to kill so efficiently but it carries the lurcher in pursuit
of the hare with the relentless urgency of the hunting
puma. I have watched this. The inevitability of the outcome, the certainty of that terrifying overhauling of one
by the other would stop a man's heart. A human mind
could barely stand the strain and the hare can see so much
more than a man! It must know death well before it comes.

The lurcher wasn't mine but when grandfather, breaking his usual habit of letting the mole-catcher or the game-
dealer have the rabbits gave its owner a line to say he could
net and snare, I hunted with it. Every morning Tam's
master would be on the scene before the milking herd was
ready to be milked or the ploughman was watering his
team. He was there for breakfast it was thought, but I
knew differently. He came to 'look' his snares or a trap he
had in a hole in the drystone wall. He sometimes came to
drive a rabbit or a hare to a net he had rigged the previous
night. When he had the right to take the rabbits he stole a
good bit of the time he was paid to do grandfather's work
so that he could block the bolt holes of hares and rabbits in
order to get them with a gate net. This was proper lurcher's
work. It requires above all else a dog used to going out

and round, an animal that works a field in the dark the way a sheepdog searches for thorn-fast ewes, slowly and methodically covering the ground. Everyone round about must have known that the lurcher was out, but for once it was legal and at least while it went on there couldn't be poaching elsewhere. We went up to the 'slaps', between the cornfield and the hayfield. A slap is a sort of barrier of larch poles, four or five of them 'threaded' through a set of horseshoes driven into gateposts on either side of a gap in a wall or a fence. The gate net is larger than a five-barred gate, deeper than the gate, and wider to allow plenty of material to entangle anything that rushes underneath. It is held in place on the top pole or bar by means of a series of stones about the size of a man's fist. The lower end of the net is tucked in under the gate and held in place there by another set of stones slightly heavier than the ones at the top. A hare or a rabbit will rush under the gate and bring the net down about itself. The man keeping watch throws himself upon the 'bag' and secures it, kills what he has taken, and puts the net back again. This must be done as quietly as possible or other game that has found no bolt holes in the field will turn back and try to dodge the lurcher.

We took perhaps five minutes to rig the net. All the stones had been selected beforehand. The lurcher was sent out and we didn't see him after he slid over the dry-stone wall. Perhaps a quarter of an hour had elapsed when the net came down with a clatter of stones. A hare was there in the grey light of a clouded moon. The net went back in place but nothing else came through the gateway until Tam arrived. His owner told me that all the signs indicated that the hares were in the corn. We had worked the dog in the hay but this was all we could do. Grandfather was a most observant man. He would have noticed that the lurcher had worked the cornfield, breaking a lot of straw and losing a lot of oats, and he would have been furious.

It was much later that autumn when we went out to long net the side of the planting with the lurcher. The corn had been cut. The hillside simply moved with rabbits because this had been a 'sown out field', which means that clover and grass seed had been sown with the final crop of oats. Now the aftergrowth was rising rich and lush. Even if we disturbed a few rabbits when the net was unfolded and pegged out there would be scores of them sitting out in little hollows in the clover clumps until the lurcher made his silent way across the hill and began working down to the fir plantation. My heart never beat faster than on these occasions. I could imagine the lurcher going and the rabbits picking the scent of him from the breeze, hopping a few yards down the hill and standing with their ears erect, fear generating in them. I could see what the owl saw, the faint haze of mist that would settle as dew, the blackness of a thorn tree along the drystone wall, and all the time the dark shadow of the dog going out, back and across again until all the rabbits moved downhill, gathering speed. Silence is what is needed, I remember being told. A man doing this kind of thing should convince himself that the thing he wants to catch might hear even his heart beating. I believe it. To be silent and move slowly means success. The lurcher took his time and its owner lay chewing on a stalk of grass until the hand on the rope supporting the long net felt the vibration caused by the first of dozens of rabbits hitting the net. Then he was on his feet and rushing about like someone demented, picking up rabbits, chopping them with the side of his hand and throwing them down to seize another. I am afraid I wasn't a lot of help. I was too worried about the net being brought down for that would have been a disaster. The lurcher appeared in front of me with a rabbit in his mouth. He let me have it and ran off. I suppose it was one of many that had tried to save themselves by crouching in the stubbles.

The mist had formed beads of moisture on my jacket and I was feeling the cold by the time it was all over. The tiresome part of the operation was the gathering up of stakes and the rolling up of the net which somehow also gathered all kinds of debris, thistles, hanks of straw and bits of dead bracken pulled out by the roots. The lurcher sat waiting for us and didn't run off to hunt in the wood which surprised me, but then he knew his job. He was like a man who had been to work and knew he had earned his keep. His owner didn't give him a second glance but spent all his time coupling the legs of the rabbits which he counted in pairs to calculate what the outing would bring in. I forget how much he said it was worth. I would have given him my share, had I been entitled to a share in the first place, if he would have let me have his dog, but that he would never have done. I have gone through life wishing I had had a lurcher but never owning one.

4

Shepherd Dog

EVERY summer there were two important events in the shepherd's calendar, shearing and dipping. For both the sheep had to be brought in from the hill and penned. In the pens they would be shorn by hand. There was no such thing as an electric shearing outfit in those days. Almost every farmer who had sheep did his own shearing or enlisted the aid of shepherds who were free to take a day's work. The business of dipping meant taking the flock to the troughs where they were steered through a series of passages and gates until they had to plunge into the unpleasant smelling trough of sheepdip. The smell of the dip was something I can remember yet. Even the taste of it lingers. It was a poison but even with all the plunging and splashing it rarely touched one's lips and more often got in the eyes. The movement of the black-face flock was engineered by the sheepdog and began early on the day of operations when the dog was sent out to bring the sheep down. This was something a good dog did with no human aid whatsoever so long as the gates had been opened. 'Bring down the sheep then,' someone would say, and the dog would leave at a canter, pacing himself for the long run away across the first field and then up the brow of the second. Sometimes he went through the gap in the wall and on to the far hill, out of sight of the steading altogether.

He worked the way any other trusted employee worked on his own and out of sight. I loved to see the sheep come, like a flood running over a hill, pouring down the way a stream runs, a little to the right and turning a little to the left again, winding a little here and there across intermediate areas of comparatively flat ground, and then steeply down again. The vanguard of them looked like a small tidal wave that swept everything before it and drowned the small creatures of the long grass. Occasionally a covey of partridges or a solitary pipit or skylark would rise before the flood and speed away. The collie would be far behind, keeping them moving, turning back and streaking to head off a straggler who had turned back. This is the sheepdog's work, of course, and when it does it it needs no instruction or even as much as a signal from the shepherd. The amazing thing about the sheepdog is that it has this thing about it, even as a pup it knows the way. It may be idle-minded and inclined at first to dawdle and play. It has its childhood and its brief adolescence when it tries its will against authority, but before long it accepts the world and knows what its work is and loves it. There are thousands of people in the world who never advance this far! There are tens of thousands who need overseers because they never learn anything.

A good sheepdog is an almost priceless animal. Fifty years ago a very good one might have brought twenty-five pounds but only a wealthy man had twenty pounds and lambs were so cheap that it was often hardly worth the shepherd's while taking them to the mart. The best shepherds were the moorland shepherds who counted their flock by hundreds, while others, the farmers who went in for sheep and cattle and a mixture of stock and arable, counted theirs in tens. The best sheepdogs came from the moors where the shepherds, between lambing and shearing, could find some time to train dogs. They did this in a variety of ways, some of them not very gentle and one or two of them cruel. We had at least one moorland sheepdog, a Border collie bred from a champion. With only a small flock of sheep even the descendant of trials winners couldn't compete with the sheepdog of the moors who every hour of every day worked over rocks and peat hags, through the sphagnum bogs and forests of dark green myrtle. The moorland dog was always lean and never over fed. It always moved like a black shadow, appearing first to the right and then to the left, coming up out of a hollow, slumping onto haunches and forepaws and watching with the frightening intensity of a wild thing. Not a generation but a thousand dog generations lie behind such animals and their acute awareness of the slightest movement or panic in a flock. Man is a clumsy, stumbling, slow-witted creature compared with such dogs and all he has is the power to make them serve his will. He would die trying to keep up with an old ram leading a flock over a heather bank. He would burst his heart in a race for the top of the hill where the escaping tail end of the flock might be turned. His mind might reach out to the distant wall where the sheep bumped over the tumbled stones, but he couldn't stop them with his will nor be there within half an hour of the last of them bumping away down through the gorse bushes, heading for the back of beyond. A peasant dog, a bond servant, a slave is the sheepdog on the moor, but he is also his master's companion and quite unaware of the fact that he is exploited and made cruel use of at times. This too, goes away back in the generations of shepherd and sheepdog. No outsider can really know the relationship between the two. It is the same as the relationship between the Cossack and his horse. The shepherd knows only a few men. His work keeps him on the moor or the mountain almost every daylight hour of every day. He knows his dog as well as he knows his wife and sometimes better. They spend all their time together, watching one another and co-operating with each other. I have watched the shepherds at work and know this association of man and dog is the closest thing possible between living creatures of a different species. Now that the horse has gone, the whisperers have died or forgotten the horseman's secret and the word, there remains only the bond between man and dog. The strongest example is that between the collie and his master. Let them call that shaggy buffoon an old English sheepdog and include the long-nosed, beautiful Shetland a dog for sheep but there really is only one breed and that is the common collie, Welsh or Border.

Old Duggie who lived in the cothouse at our road end had a very fine sheepdog, a dog of great intelligence that was nimble on its feet but shy of strangers and never given to greeting them by even the slightest twitch of its tail. I loved to see our sheep and Duggie's milling together down at the dipping pens, seeing the blue and red rump or shoulder marks getting mixed up and the two collies standing off at a respectable distance, aware of one another, bristling a little but each of them at work and not able to skirmish. The sheep would go right through the pens and the trough mixed up, and everyone would lend a hand wearing sackcloth aprons and leggings—the leather, strap-on legging shaped to fit the calf was popular with ploughmen in those days. When they helped at the dipping the leggings saved them from getting too wet. Wellingtons were treacherous things to wear in the pens when they were greasy with trodden droppings and awash with dip draining from the fleeces of the sheep. No one talked of 'his' sheep and 'our' sheep when this work was done and the policeman brought out his forms to testify that the law had been complied with. The sheep shuddered and shook themselves. Dip flew from their fleeces. The sun dried them. As soon as they could the dogs would be whistled up and given their orders to sort out one lot from the other. Although they may not have known the markings they knew their own sheep, just as the shepherd knows the members of his flock and almost imperceptibly 'his' sheep and 'our' sheep would be segregated once more. It always fascinated me to see this done with only the odd stray to be caught up with a crook about her neck and hauled over to join her own lot.

When the sheep were brought from the hill to be looked for maggot or checked for footrot, if such a pest had contaminated the ground, it might be noticed when a count was taken that one or two were missing. The dog lying on his belly back on the short grass of the home paddock would lift his head and wait to be told. A moment later he would be away in search of the missing ones. Sometimes one of these sheep would be tied in a big bramble clump growing out of a stone heap or held fast in a ditch overgrown by thorns and dog rose. When this happened the dog would come and show himself on the hill and trot back to the place where a particular sheep stood panting with flies about its head and weeds draped about its small curled horns. Perhaps it was telepathy that would make the dog try just once more to force the sheep to struggle to free itself. Often this final effort freed the ewe and she would trot out onto the field. She would meander in the direction of the rest of the flock while the dog went on to find another one similarly caught up or perhaps bogged in the peat away up by the march fence and the rowan trees. What is a clever dog but one that does what man wants of it? I have never been quite sure, but sometimes the dog is cleverer than the man. I have seen a sheepdog sitting waiting for help to come when it might have frightened a bogged sheep and caused it to sink deeper into the peat.

As a family grandfather's household had the greatest respect for the working dog and the sheepdog in particular and yet I remember when a renegade sheepdog was seen running along the slope opposite the kitchen having left behind him five or six dead and dying ewes. It was the spring of the year, a time when this kind of thing happens to all sorts and sizes of dogs. There were only a few pet dogs for miles around. In the main the dogs that were kept were sheep dogs, dogs for cattle and of course, the keeper's dog and the poacher's lurcher. Here was a working dog gone wrong, and there, at the corner of the old stackyard field was evidence of murder. Father and I were at home on this occasion. Grandfather looked out at the running dog and his face was grim. 'You will take the gun and shoot that dog when he comes back to the sheep to-morrow!' he told father. Father looked depressed. The very thought of shooting a dog is enough to depress most of us. The following morning, as was almost inevitable, the wandering killer was seen down in the same corner, tearing at one of his victims of the day before, since all the rest of the flock had been moved to a safe place near the steading.

'Get the gun!' said grandfather. I suppose he didn't appoint himself executioner because he was lame and not fast enough on his feet to gain a few yards on a worrying dog making off for the wall. Father got the gun and loaded it. I ran with him, not because I wanted to see the dog shot, but to see if father could do what he had been ordered to do. We went through the gate one behind the other. Father ran half-heartedly and I kept pace. The dog that was tearing great clumps of fleece from the dead sheep didn't see us at first. We were almost within gunshot before he knew we were there. When he saw us he stopped with his mouth fast in the fleece and his legs braced. All at once he let go and whirled about to streak for the wall. Father put up the gun, swung with the running dog. He hardly ever missed what he aimed at in those days. His co-ordination was perfect. He was fast and accurate, but I saw him let the gun hang before he pulled the trigger. The shot bounced off the ground twelve feet or more behind the dog. The dog itself cleared the wall like a wolf and went on up the far field until it was lost to sight in a fold of the ground. We went back to the kitchen. Grandfather didn't need to be told what had happened.

'Five ewes,' he said heavily. It wasn't really a reproach. Perhaps he could have shot the dog in hot blood, but he would have done what father had done. I was quite sure of that. Father took care not to be on hand when there was any danger of the sheep-worrier coming back. The household was divided. One of my aunts was really the shepherd and had all money from the flock and the sale of wool or lambs. She was for shooting and might have shot the dog herself, but the rest, including grandfather were on the fence, or on the other side of it. The situation didn't arise again. Everyone round about knew the dog, although its owner didn't or wouldn't own it and made no protest when, one morning it ran through a neighbour's flock and came face to face with the shepherd who just happened to have left his crook at home and carried a gun instead. A man must advertise before he shoots a dog, they said, but there was no time for that. The dog died in his tracks. There was blood on his muzzle and a dead ewe on the grazing behind him. It was more like a wolf than a shepherd's dog.

5

Cry Help

Dogs are given all kinds of names, some of them as un-
suitable as the names their owners chose for their houses
but in general working dogs have short names which can
be easily enunciated so that the dog will understand that
it is being addressed. I have known a score of shepherd
dogs called Meg, Tam, Bess and Jackie, but there were
others kept by the family that showed a little originality.
There was Help. I suppose someone gave the pup this
name so that everyone who heard the dog called for the
first time would look puzzled and then smile. How many
hundreds of times have I heard the injunction, 'Cry Help!'
when a pig was in the corn or a bullock busily tucking into
a hayrick and likely to bore right on through it unless
moved by the dog. Help was another born-old collie. There
were a great many of his kind about the farms of south-
west Scotland when I was a child, dogs almost identical in
colouring and marking. He was shaggy, short-nosed,
black with a white brand at his neck. He was a little stiff
in his movements like an ageing farm labourer, which he
was, I suppose. He didn't hurry but assessed every task for
himself and dog-trotted to do what was needed, telling
himself that he must get a move on if sheep were about to
pour away through a hole in the hedge. It was no use telling him to get after them. He paid little heed to shouted

commands. He knew what had to be done. Shouted commands were a kind of hysteria which some humans suffered
from. He had no time for people of that sort. He wasn't a
smiling dog, if you know what that means. I don't think
I ever saw him looking pleased with himself or remotely
self-satisfied. When he had done his task he ran at heel.
When he was no longer needed he trotted in and took his
favourite place behind the long table and under a 'form' or
bench that stood against the wall there. He would lie with
his tail curled round and his nose just touching his hind
feet and he slept. Sometimes he opened his eyes and listened
to what was being said. If there was talk of work for him
he became alert. If the tone of voice was low, the drone of
bedtime conversation, he settled for the night. No one as
much as touched the sneck of the door once the oil lamp
was out without being startled by Help's deep-chested
bark. That bark would come up the well of the stairs and
bring those who were abed onto their elbows, listening. It
used to awaken me when I had a downstairs bedroom and I
would be suddenly afraid that someone was trying to lift
the casement window, the catch of which had been broken
long before I was born. Perhaps the disturbance wasn't
some itinerant tramp trying the door of a lonely farmhouse
but a young ploughman tramping home from an evening
with his sweetheart and passing through our court on his
way. Help wasn't a savage dog. He was too cool in every
way to be provoked into attacking a man, but when he
thought there was someone about who shouldn't have
been there a rumble began in his shaggy throat. He barked
with the full power of his lungs, once twice and on and on
until the night seemed to be punctuated by the sound. All
at once he would fall silent, having listened between barks
and decided that whatever had come had gone again. The
family would slip into deep sleep knowing that Help slept
lightly.

It wasn't the custom to go visiting or even to cross a
neighbour's land with a dog for company unless the dog

was being taken for some particular purpose, to herd back
a sow that had been earlier taken to the boar or steer a stray
sheep home after it had been culled from someone's flock.
The keeper too, was always on the lookout for people
crossing his territory with a dog, especially a dog running
free. He would complain and make dire threats about what
he would do if the dog came within range of his gun. Help
wasn't by any stretch of imagination a poaching dog or
even one given to marking sleeping hares or looking sideways at a bolting rabbit. He was a completely responsible
dog, fit to be taken anywhere. He would have trotted
behind his master through burning gorse or heather, I am
sure, and wouldn't have batted an eye at praise for having
done so. I think he was a cynical dog. He had seen it all.
He had it all summed up. He knew all the weaknesses and
all the cunning ways of humans. Had he been a man and
in the army he would never have volunteered. He would
have refused a lance corporal's stripe and never played pon-
toon. Again I will be accused of anthromoporphic self-
delusion, but I claim again that some of the characteristics
we attribute to man have been equally cultivated in animals
that have lived with him. A dog is a very good judge of
human nature. I see no reason to suggest that it isn't influenced by what it sees and knows of the ways of man.
Help was a disconcertingly human kind of dog. He really
was like an old employee. He wasn't particularly bright.
He was a plodder. He was completely reliable and he
earned his keep. I won't go so far as to say that he had an
inkling of the meaning of the words 'overtime' or 'day
of rest' but he knew when he had earned a rest, and he
knew it was wise to lie up and take his ease when there was
a lull.

Both my aunts set great store by Help's being around
when the men were working out in the fields, perhaps cutting the 'wee five-acre' or making hay down on the side
of the bog. The summer days were long and when the
sun shone it was possible to get on with hay-making or

corn cutting. A drowsy peace would settle over the steading. Hens would dust-bath and old sows lie on the grass with their litters struggling to feed. Help would be out by the door or in under the form. If a gipsy cart came trundling up the road and the travelling people knocked on the door to press the womenfolk to buy tea towels or something of the sort Help could be relied upon to rise, stiff on his legs, and stand beside them when they shook their heads and tried to close the door. If a tramp came with his tea-can begging first tea, and then sugar and finally milk, he was soon aware that he was being watched. He had no way of knowing that Help was unlikely to as much as bare his fangs. Indeed, looking at the dog's grim, black face and the stiff way he stood with the hair ruffed behind his collar it often seemed that he was a most ferocious creature who would have a man down and rip and tear him. 'Cry Help,' one of my aunts would urge the other, 'here comes that old Snib Scott again,' and when Snib came loping up with his tea-can, looking no less disreputable because he was wearing an old army greatcoat on a hot summer's day, Help would be on hand. There were some farms where alarm dogs were kept chained in open-sided sheds, ferocious beasts that leapt to the full extent of their tether, showing yellow fangs and snarling like mad things. Here there was only the house dog, one of the family. His bark was more than his bite. Hardly anyone ever saw him bite, except my Aunt Mary and my great-uncle's family who had a farm a mile or so away. Help was responsible for an estrangement that was nothing short of a feud that wasn't settled in a lifetime.

It happened when my aunt decided to pay a call on our relatives and opted to walk across the fields and the rough gorse grown land that separated us from Capenoch where great-uncle Peter lived. For some reason Mary felt the need for company. She had crossed that ground at almost every hour of the day or night on previous occasions. She knew every boulder and stone on the way and what she might encounter going over the march wall or walking the bank above the deep peat drain. There was no danger of anyone intercepting her but she called Help and took him with her. Help obeyed. Perhaps he felt he was entitled to an evening without having to bark the milkers down the road. He trotted at heel and only now and then went ahead to lead his mistress. They came at last to the farm road and great uncle Peter's small holding. The resident collie barked them greeting and came stiff-legged to sniff at Help and they all went to the farmhouse together. Aunt Mary talked of this and that, the prospects for harvest, the way the hay had turned out, the hens going off the lay and her hopes of making raspberry jam—the usual topics of conversation between country people in those days. Great-uncle Peter toiled in his small fields, getting in his hay the hard way with only one horse to pull his cart up the steep brow and his children his only helpmates. When visitors came it was the custom to lay out the best china, the silver cakestand loaded with shortbread, plates of pancakes and scones, the cream jug and the silver teapot. Hospitality demanded it and the family would have been shamed to think that it hadn't been done. The feast was spread and great-uncle Peter and his helpers summoned to it. They came as excited as a family on a picnic and the scones and shortbread began to be devoured, the red gooseberry jam licked from sticky fingers. Everyone talked at once and laughed, until all at once the table began to shake, the dishes danced, a cream jug fell over, the teapot crashed onto the floor. Help and great-uncle Peter's dog were at one another's throats! Children screamed and everyone fell back from the table, frightened, dismayed and in danger as the dogs whirled and snarled and bit. Aunt Mary's little black eyes opened in alarm. She gaped at the dogs with their teeth sunk in one another's throats, and then, seizing a brush which just happened to be standing by the grand-father clock, she jumped in and began to belabour the dog that was killing 'our poor Help'. This proved too much for

great-uncle Peter. He couldn't stand by and watch his dog
not only being savaged but beaten down by an angry little
woman with a brush in her hands. He picked up his walking stick and began to redress the balance, giving Help as
many blows as Aunt Mary was giving his dog. The table
cloth was dragged from the table, cups in fragments littered
the floor. Biscuits and shortbread were trodden into the
tiles. There was bedlam and nothing the contestants did
seemed likely to bring the thing to a conclusion until great
uncle Peter's wife picked up the watercan and drenched
the two dogs. The snarling ceased. Aunt Mary caught
Help by the collar and gently pulled him to the door. She
looked grimly at her uncle. 'You had no right to belabour
this poor dog like that!' she said bitterly. 'It will be a long
time before either of us crosses your door again!'
Great-uncle Peter had the family temper. He glared at his
niece. She had dared to abuse him. She had allowed her
dog to savage his. She had been the cause of the whole
thing, bringing the unbiddable animal in the first place
when there was no need to bring a dog. Uncle Peter himself would never have dreamed of coming visiting with a
dog at his heels!

All this was lost on Aunt Mary. She was affronted. She
couldn't forgive the blows inflicted upon good, faithful
Help, and she never would. She had used the brush on her
uncle's dog but only to prevent it killing Help, who was a
peaceful, good dog, never known to bite or attack anyone.
She turned on her heel and Help fell in behind her. They
hurried down the road and back across the rough fields to
the marches of home to tell grandfather what had befallen
them.

'God knows,' said the old man, 'there's no need to take
a dog to a tea party! What was he going for? Was there
anything for him to do?'

The question didn't really need to be asked but Aunt
Mary, whose mind was quick, had an answer. She had
taken Help so that on the way home he could bring the

cows off the hill for milking. She didn't bother to say that by the time she did get back the milking was half done and had the tea party reached a peaceful conclusion she might have stayed and played a hand of whist or helped prepare fruit for the making of jam. Neither Aunt Mary nor Help visited Capenoch again. The feud was one of those things that stand like milestones in the lives of a great many country people, something not to be forgotten, an embarrassment to communication as it had once been.

Help died and was buried. He would be remembered when family dogs were discussed and compared. The most frequent memory resurrected was the fight that afternoon at Capenoch, when the scones rolled and the dishes danced and 'skin and hair' flew. With the passing of time the whole thing became embellished and embroidered. It might have lasted an hour but probably only lasted five minutes. In that time their were tears and exclamations of dismay and indignation, and a lot of highly-prized tea-cups, plates and saucers were cracked and broken. It was the only time, as far as I am aware, that old Help behaved like a dog. Was he attacked or did he make the first move? Well, he was one of us. I would say that he was attacked. He was really all for the quiet life. He was far too sane to start such a brawl in his own house, or anyone else's.

6

Poor Tweed

THE life of a working dog is short, especially a dog that is
out in all weathers, earning his keep by shepherding. The
dog's coat gets wet and only his continual exertions dry the
long hair on most occasions. This is not to say that shepherds are callous towards their dogs. It is impossible to
mollycoddle a dog that travels twenty miles on a wet or
damp and misty day. The dog steams out by the fire. The
onset of rheumatism is inevitable. His master almost
certainly suffers from it himself. They are both used to
sheltering and shivering on the lea sides of drystone walls
or close under a dripping peat bank that shields them from
the wind. A procession of dogs accompanied me through
my childhood and adolescence. I would come back on
holiday and find the faces changed and a new dog there
being trained. I suppose most of these faithful animals had
a working life of six or seven years and were pensioned off
but where they all came from I was never able to find out.
I suppose my grandfather met a hill shepherd at the market
and arranged to buy a useful or partly-trained dog and
there were more where this one came from. Tweed may
have been one of these. Grandfather was reckoned to be a
very good judge of horseflesh. He bred some good Clydes-
dales and I suppose in a lifetime he must have acquired an
eye for a dog, but dogs weren't his business by any stretch

of imagination. He once in a while bought the wrong horse (and quickly got rid of it again) and he should have done this with poor Tweed, but there it was. Tweed came at the wrong time, when my brothers were there to accompany me into the wilderness and we were all as wild as the hare itself. Tweed was about the same mental age, a young dog, not sure what life was meant to be about. He was there to be trained and he no more wanted training than I wanted the schoolroom. He wanted to be free. I suppose the only people he understood were children. The old working dog looked upon him with disapproval and often nipped him for some misdemeanour or out of downright meanness. He wanted to escape and hated to be made to stand by in case he might be needed. When we were off for the morning he would slip out after us, slinking up the hedgeside and only attaching himself to us when he thought he wouldn't be sent home. We didn't send him home unless we encountered one of the family, an adult who commanded us to send him home. As soon as he discovered that we were the next best thing to a pack of hunting dogs, Tweed was our inseparable companion. He would follow us anywhere. He taught himself to hunt with us, to co-operate in the jungle way of beating through a great gorse clump to drive out a hare that had foolishly taken shelter there instead of racing off across the open ground. There was never anything that made my hackles rise as much as this tension. Tweed's hair ruffed too. He would pause and look at us and words were no longer necessary. A moment later the hare would bolt and we would throw our sticks to bring him down if we could. Sometimes it wasn't a hare that came out but an old cock pheasant, running as fast as any hare, and arrowing for the shelter of a bank or a thicket to which we would all charge like savages to renew the hunt. Often these prolonged chases ended with our quarry crossing a deep drain or taking to the air with a great clatter as cock pheasants will. Tweed and his accomplices would slow down for a hundred yards or so until a rabbit was startled out of the round rushes and bolted for a bush a few yards farther on. We knew every warren and almost every burrow in every warren. We had Tweed to dig for us, a thing he would do almost lying on his side and using his forefeet furiously as he built a mound of black earth behind him and sometimes threw the stuff in our eyes. We had ways of smoking rabbits out by lighting little fires of gorse on the windward side of a bank and making sure the suffocating smoke was fanned into the burrow. We were barbarians and when I think of it all now I am sorry for Tweed. He came to be a sheepdog and he might have been one if he hadn't been led astray. He might never have met his executioner, I think, but for the fact that his dog youth was misspent.

'The boys are ruining that dog,' someone would say. We didn't think so. We loved him and he loved to be with us. He was wild and we were wild. No one said we were ruining ourselves. Did we corrupt him or did he corrupt us? I don't think anyone was to blame. When we ran with Tweed or he ran with us, barking and dancing round us as we sprang down from the drystone wall, we were doing what man and dog had done almost since the beginning of time. If there was any perversion of natural instinct it was in making the dog nursemaid to stupid sheep. How many days we hunted the bracken, the great sea of round rushes in the low bog, the mossy hags and heather banks, the gorse hills and long grass of the hay fields with him! Our elders were too busy to concern themselves with what was happening. Everyone had work to do, harrowing newly sown oats, cleaning out the stable, feeding hens, carting peats, mowing rushes for rickyard thatch.

We went back to London and returned again for another holiday. In London I would think of Tweed while I struggled with my homework and even when I sat in the classroom. The schoolmaster knew the idlers and the day-dreamers only too well. He would prod me with the black-board pointer when I was five hundred miles away on a

stubble hill watching a covey of partridges whirring in a
hollow and looking at Tweed when he turned and looked
at me. What did the dreary theorems of Euclid matter?
Even in the chalk dust I could breathe the scent of the
moss and follow Tweed's swaying tail as he bustled
through scrub bushes and old, blackened gorse the shepherd had fired in spring. 'Come back to earth!' the schoolmaster would urge, and I came back to triangles and arcs
and radii. They never meant a thing to me but I did know
where you could put up a hare and Tweed knew where to
cut it off. Even if he didn't we could run on and find another
or put a rabbit out and knock him down with a stick. The
schoolmaster never knew the kind of savage he was trying
to teach. He knew the boys who lingered late at night in
the gaslight pools of almost deserted streets. He knew
those whose dreams were of finding a sixpence and going
to the pictures, but he didn't know me and if he had he
would have shuddered. In a year or two I would spend all
of every holiday wandering with a gun, fishing for trout or
looking for plovers' nests, but this was to come. I would be
put on the train back north fearful only that in the mean-
time Tweed would have been turned into a sober old working dog who couldn't be persuaded to join in and hunt the
woods, even the keeper's preserves when we knew he was
engaged elsewhere. Tweed didn't change. The damage
was done. He was a renegade. He had reverted to ancestors
back beyond his herding forebears, his servile father and
grandfather. His failure as a working dog was already well-
known and accepted. When people came to visit they
would remark upon him for he was black and brown, a sort
of brindly colour, not unlike dyed Harris tweed I suppose.
The adults of the family would look at him and shrug. He
was a waster, something to be ashamed of, hidden away
like an alcoholic relative. 'The boys spoilt him,' they
would say. They didn't mean that he had been spoiled as a
child is indulged, but ruined. Poor Tweed knew it. He
would creep in under the table, aware of the shame. We

were sorry for him. The world was cruel. All he wanted to do was to enjoy his young life. His development had been arrested, I suppose a psychiatrist might say. He had been turned into a permanent adolescent.

When we couldn't hunt the fields because it was too wet or too cold even for the hardiest of us, there was always a cat hunt. The farm had more than its share of cats. They were never the sleek, well-fed cats of the old ladies but lean and hungry, Cassius cats that lived by their wits. They had tattered ears and patches of baldness on their heads or backs. They growled more than they purred. They snarled and sprang at one another like angry tigers. A misguided compassion made my aunts put out churn lids of milk for these wild strays. They said it was by way of reward for all the mice and rats they must kill, but come threshing day there were always just as many mice and rats in the rick bottoms. We hunted these hungry cats in a wild stampede from stable to barn and high granary, from the open-sided shed to the piggery and up the byre walks. If anyone heard us yelling in pursuit they would come out and give us a lecture that would leave us all with hanging heads. Only Tweed escaped, for he would be off on the top of the hay or the at back of the straw house, cornering one of those spitting, long-clawed wild cats in the hope that we might eventually come up with him. It was all very reprehensible. It had to stop. Father lectured us and threatened us with all kinds of punishment. Grandfather raged as only he could. Tweed was forbidden to hunt. We were forbidden ever to take him to the fields again, or hiss him on to chase the most scabby of the cat intruders. It wasn't just cruel. It was the ruin of a dog. His end would come, tied to a stake and looking up at the barrels of a twelve-bore.

Poor Tweed slunk about with his tail between his legs. When we went away he began to take himself hunting. People reported him far and wide, loping along a wall like a wolf, standing all by himself on some big field of feathery ryegrass and looking guilty as a sheep-worrier, which was the only crime he hadn't yet committed. It wasn't just that he roamed and neighbours saw their flocks crowding in a corner as he passed, but that he was recognized as our dog. This was like one of the family making a fool of himself in public, at market or on a cattle show day. His name was the family's name. He had to be chained and kept in the stable. There was nothing else for it. I have felt guilty about it ever since but what is one dog more or less some people will say? Man is a superior animal and dogs are expendable.

It happened that Tweed had been kept on the chain so long that although he had a fine bed of dry straw and could sleep the clock round and find his food dish full, he became morose. He began to snarl at those who came near him. The chain held him in the manger. He saw nothing. He heard very little except the horses grinding their oats and the cock crowing. It was wrong and someone should have done something about it. A young cousin came into the stable for something one day and walked past poor sleeping Tweed who came awake in a frenzy of rage, leapt up and tore at him. The boy staggered back with a frightful wound on his upper lip. The doctor had to stitch it. There was even some anxiety in case such a wild, roaming dog could have contracted rabies. They did what had become inevitable. Tweed was taken on the end of the chain and led to the place of execution where a hole had been dug and a pile of quicklime tipped from a cauldron. The chain was fastened to a stake. Tweed crouched on all fours and looked at the farmhand with the gun. He surely knew in that moment where his life had finally led him, or perhaps he didn't. Perhaps he wondered why the gun came to bear on his head and was steadied for a moment. The shot echoed back from the walls of the steading and Tweed slumped, blood colouring his black and tan head. His body was tipped into the pit and the lime shovelled in on top with a long-handled lime shovel. When I came on holiday again I saw the place where he was buried. The stake was still in the ground. I choked a little and wiped a tear from my cheek because he had been part of my boyhood and my brothers' boyhood too. He had been as close a companion as any of us had known and we had brought him to this.

Grandfather was philosophical about it. A dog bites a man and he must be put down, he said. Mind you, the man was often as much to blame as the dog, whether he was aware of it or not. This is the truth of it. A dog bites because he is frightened, because he is driven out of his mind, because he has been brutally used. We can find in it all the reasons we find for human misdeeds. We make our dogs what they are. It is a long time since Tweed was shot. No other dog the family had was 'put down', as country folk call it. I can't forget him. I hunt with him still, not because I long for the wildness, but because I would love to know again the exhilaration, the tense excitement of the days we ran wild together, young and free as the wind blowing across the moss. It saddens me when I look at myself past middle-age and at my brothers and know how impossible it is for us to ever know such excitement again.

7

The Old Man's Darling

JACKIE was the dog that was left behind, inconsolable
when his master died. Grandfather talked to him as he
talked to humans, I always felt. At least he would tell
Jackie what he had to do, or, when Jackie would be off to
amuse himself or greet the dog of someone coming visiting
he would bid him lie still and Jackie obeyed. He was either
close beside the old man's chair or lying across his route
to the door. They always went out together but the domestic arrangements didn't permit Jackie to lie on the sitting-
room floor, unless he could sneak in there and lie low when
the womenfolk came down after supper. He was never
allowed in the parlour in any case. Working collies are not
over-groomed. In fact they are left to groom themselves
more often than not and when they get wet they tend to
have what is called a doggy smell by refined and dog-loving
old ladies. One of my aunts had no sense of smell whatever
(she was the one who prepared the hare for the pot!) but
the other was in no way afflicted and could detect poor
Jackie even when he had sidled away in behind a settee in
the overcrowded sitting room. Invariably Jackie was
flushed out and left for the kitchen with a look of sadness
on his normally cheerful face. Jackie was a young-in-spirit
dog and not one of the sober old fellows often employed
in the past. He was the most intelligent of the 'herds', and

44

so he should have been because he came of a famous strain. Bess, his mother had been a great champion. She had actually penned her blackfaces in Hyde Park, it was said (or was it Windsor?), before no less a person than His Majesty George V. She must have been in great demand when shepherds were seeking good litters from which to buy pups. Grandfather indulged himself when he bought Jackie for the price would have been high, too high for the man who wasn't really a sheep farmer at all, but kept no more than a 100 to 150 blackfaces. The wonder of it all was that Jackie was properly trained into the bargain. No semi-skilled, novice shepherd took him in hand to make him good enough for a small flock on a mixed farm, but a moorland expert. When he had done with him Jackie came to work exclusively for one master, which is another of the secrets of dog-control. Grandfather knew how important it was to have one master for a horse or a dog. Jackie took his orders only from his master. Anyone else coming upon the scene and giving orders to Jackie was ignored by the dog and frowned upon by grandfather, sometimes even cursed for daring to speak! Jackie was like the laird's factor or bailiff. He had his master's ear, it seemed. Often when someone had driven or ridden the old man's pony he would announce that the pony had told him that he had been misused or abused. He would say this quite seriously and accusingly, and I am sure there was some communication between him and his favourite pony. The same applied to Jackie. The family had only to look at the way the dog kept his eyes on the old man to know that he adored him, was jealous of anyone who went near him, and would almost certainly have died for him. It makes me sad to recall that Jackie outlived his master. This happens when a man replaces one dog with another all through his life. One of them is bound to be left to mourn.

Jackie's ability to understand every word that was said might have been questioned by those who have studied the extent to which dogs understand the meaning of commands and the way they associate certain words with certain things. It is a complex business, communication between man and animal. Half of it depends upon the visual. Once at least I saw it demonstrated that Jackie understood words other than commands and needed no gesture to indicate what was expected of him. I was on holiday from London at this time. The corn was ripening and harvest was at hand. Every day grandfather would take a walk to consider the state of his cornfields and the question of opening roads for the binder. This required some judgement of the weather to come, and the degree of green still streaking the sea of oats in different parts of the field. It entailed pulling a head or two and fingering the grain, and grandfather loved this moment because it was the very climax of a long period of labour, ploughing, harrowing, rolling the oats and now pronouncing them ready for the binder. We walked up the old road past the stackyard. The stone 'butts' of the ricks—round boulders arranged in circles upon which the sheaves of oats would be built—had all been gone over. The stackyard was tidy and waiting for the corn to be cut and gathered. On the other side of the road there was a small field of oats, a less important field than the switchback or the big hill where the acreage was much greater and the corn, out of the sun, took longer to ripen. As we went up the road grandfather spotted one of the old brood sows in the field on our left. He would have her out of that, but before he did more than quietly say 'Watch this,' he put his hand on my arm and made sure of my attention. Very quietly he spoke to the dog, his tone neither urgent nor commanding. 'Jackie,' he said, 'there's an old sow in the corn. You had better put her out.' Jackie sprang onto the drystone wall and dropped into the standing corn. In a minute he was out there turning the sow and steering her back the way she had come, giving her a little nip on the heels to keep her jog-trotting.

'You saw how he did that?' the old man asked. 'Would

you say he went because I ordered him? Did I point my stick? Did he jump the right way? He didn't go into the stackyard, did he?' I had to admit that the dog seemed to have understood exactly what his master had said and had done exactly what was required of him. The disconcerting thought so far as I was concerned was how much the dog understood. It would have been something other than vocal communication—telepathy. Jackie had been trained to work to the whistle as all sheepdogs are trained, but so many of the things he did for the old man needed neither whistle nor word. Grandfather wasn't a complicated man. He was a simple countryman not given to searching his soul or being particularly introvert, any more than he was extrovert. He was quite convinced that he could talk to horses and horses did remarkable things for him. Jackie was a dog with whom he established the same strange affinity. In his old age, like many another old man grandfather probably felt that communication was diminishing. The world doesn't really listen to old men because they are concerned with the past, whether it may have been successful or unsuccessful. The young man anticipates his future. He lives tomorrow and can't wait for it to come. What the old man says about yesterday is not a great deal of help in solving problems that will arise tomorrow. Living is change and nothing stays the same to be solved by yesterday's remedy. As he neared his end grandfather became fonder of his dog. Even old men when they meet rarely want to hear what the others have to say. Jackie didn't argue. Jackie put his bright, intelligent head on the old man's knee and his look told the old man he was important. He mattered, if only to his dog. They went out to the hill and studied the rolling countryside in which grandfather had spent all his life. They came in and had their breakfast, grandfather cutting the crust from his bread and dipping it in the yolk of his egg to give it to Jackie. They went round the steading and Jackie watched his master examine the foot of a mare that was likely to cast a shoe, or helped him move pigs so that the man could clean the piggery. The days passed like this. When the old man took his afternoon nap his dog would sleep on the cold waxcloth that covered the passage leading to the stairs and sighed if anyone ordered him to move.

I wasn't there when grandfather died and arrived on the following day in response to a telephoned message. Everyone was in a state of shock and yet his death was as peaceful and somehow fitting as his own father's death had been. Great grandfather had been in bed, not seriously ill, but a little tired. He had asked for his pipe and had sat up and smoked it with great contentment, announced that he would take a 'wee sleep' and closed his eyes for the final long sleep. Grandfather too had left his pipe on the bedside table and turned on his side. When he didn't come tapping his way downstairs at his usual hour, one of my aunts looked at the clock, thinking to go up and awaken him. At that moment Jackie stood up and raised his head and howled painfully before rushing out of the house. My aunts knew, without going up the stair, that grandfather had died. The doctor was summoned, of course, and said that he had died of old age and had simply worn out, like a piece of machinery that has worked for a long time. Jackie didn't come back but stayed out in the fields. It was a bleak spring and bitterly cold at night. No one had time to go and search for him. I doubt whether he would have responded to anyone trying to cajole him to come home. His master was dead. He hadn't needed to be there in the room to know that his heart had ceased to beat. No one knew until Jackie howled that anything that afternoon was different from any other afternoon. Dogs have highly developed senses. They know much more than we give them credit for, of course, but scientists have discovered sensors, reactors, highly-developed nerves that have long since atrophied or ceased to be cultivated in the human animal. They would smile at mere telepathy between cat and dog, one reacting to the other completely out of its sight. They might talk about the smell of death, about the nervous system of the dog and its sensitivity to the emanations of the human body. Jackie wasn't the first dog to howl at death. There are hundreds of legends, and probably hundreds of authenticated instances of dogs doing this. The howling isn't an invention of a writer like Edgar Alan Poe or a Conan Doyle device. I know that it happened. My aunts, one of whom is a very old lady, is alive at this moment to testify to the fact, for after he howled she went up the stairs and looked at her father's face, shook him gently, and saw that he was dead. Her sister came up after her and they stood by the bed and cried. One of them looked out through the skylight window and saw Jackie running away as fast as his legs would carry him.

Jackie came back after the funeral. He was a sad dog and never regained his spirit. They looked at him and knew he grieved. He was a mourning dog for the rest of his time. A young cousin took over the farm and ran it until he too, died, but in more tragic circumstances. My aunts moved into a lodge on the nearby estate, taking Jackie with them as well as two or three of their more domesticated cats and a canary. The cats and the dog tolerated each other. The household was a peaceful one. Occasionally the cats brought back a young rabbit they had caught in the adjoining woods but Jackie never hunted. He hadn't been brought up to that sort of thing. He was a trained sheepdog in retirement and looked disdainfully at dogs that herded cattle along the road on their way to grass parks or the market. He slept a good part of his time and his only duty was to warn his mistresses of the passing tramp or tinkers' barrows. At night he shared the hearthrug with the cats and looked at them sadly, perhaps because he had come to matter so little that cats were his equal. He understood what was said to him as well as he had understood his master. I visited the lodge once when Jackie was still alive and one of my aunts reminded me of grandfather's confidence in Jackie's ability to understand every word that was spoken. 'I'll praise the cat,' said my aunt, 'and you just listen to poor Jackie!' I looked at Jackie lying with his head on his paws. 'Isn't that a lovely cat?' my aunt said. 'Isn't she a clever cat? I love that cat!' Poor Jackie lifted his head and howled! He went on howling as long as the cat was praised. He had become insecure in his old age, I suppose, and felt that he had been supplanted in the old ladies' affection by the fat, black cat. This wasn't the case, of course. Nothing could ever take his place. They loved him dearly. He was a link with their father and somehow, as long as they had him, he was part of life as it had been.

Jackie was the last dog they owned. The last dog in a long line of faithful, working animals, helpmates who had brought cows off the pasture on wet mornings and barked them back to the meadows on sunny summer evenings, dogs that had saved them from angry bulls, protected them from vagabonds, accompanied them along the dark roads when they went visiting at night and barked a welcome when they had been away at the town shopping for a dress or visiting old friends there. They had never kept a dog as a pet. Having a pet was to make a fool of an animal, to reduce its dignity and shame man himself. They would have hotly denied that the dogs they had had were in the same category as unpaid servants and insisted they were members of the family.

8

A Dog for the House

HAVING a dog is for most people something less than keeping up with the Joneses, unless the Joneses happen to have something like an Afghan or an Irish wolfhound! When a couple are newly married they rarely place a very high priority upon having a dog. Dogs come later, to round off a family, perhaps, or to keep out the neighbourhood cats. When I was first married I was quite young and saw myself as a man of responsibility. I knew nothing at all about the business of being a householder. My approach to a burst pipe was with a handful of string, some soap and a rag. I was no great shakes as a plumber. As a home decorator my head was in the clouds because I thought all undercoat paint was grey, like cats in the dark. I happily tarred the woodwork of the room we had chosen as a nursery with battleship grey paint and airily told my wife that this was undercoat. The nursery would be whatever colour she wanted once I had undercoated! I knew about dogs, of course, working dogs and hunting dogs for marking rabbit holes. I really didn't see what people, without several acres of ground in which to exercise and use a dog, wanted one for. Undercoat may have been grey but I saw the world in black and white, north and south, honest men and liars.

The nursery wasn't needed, alas, for we lost our first

child at birth and I suppose my parents thought we needed something upon which to lavish affection. All at once they arrived at our door bringing with them a small half-cairn pup, one of a litter born to Milly, their cairn bitch. Milly was part of the family. She was talked about by her name only. No one ever thought to explain to strangers that she was a dog. They discovered this in the course of time. Poor Milly had been out and about with some of the terriers roaming loose near my father's house in Wilmslow, Cheshire, and the resulting pups had been disposed of with the exception of Jock. Jock was nothing to look at, but father assured me that he was the pick of the litter, a battling little fellow, bright-eyed and not daunted by anything or anyone.

We received the present politely. My wife was pleased, but I was not. I felt that having a dog was something everyone should decide for himself—I never did, of course and the dogs I had were all wished upon me! Very well, since he had come, we would put up with him, but we would begin as we intended to go on. He would live downstairs in a dog box. He would be well fed and he would be house-trained, or else! He would in return bark to warn us of intruders, keep away cats and never get under my feet. I didn't sit down there and then and draw up the rules, but I put them into words. Jock squirmed and wriggled and swarmed about the floor, crouched and made a puddle and generally behaved as though I didn't exist. I felt like a Hyde Park orator whose audience had melted away. My wife wiped up the pools and told the wobbly-legged creature with the coconut matting coat that he couldn't help it, and he would learn, wouldn't he? I said with great menace that he had better learn, hadn't he? And another thing, he seemed already prone to chewing every thing he came across. That too, would come to an end. We retired for the night, very firmly shutting the scullery and then the kitchen door to keep the six-week-old monster from breaking through to the stairs and the bedroom above. He was a crafty little monster however. He knew he couldn't open two doors and climb stairs. He began to weep from about half-past ten or eleven o'clock, and he wept continually for at least half an hour. I cursed him with great fury and put my head under the bedclothes. My wife sat up and suggested that she might go down. I forbade her to do any such thing. We would begin the way we intended to go on. Give in now and the little brute would cry every night. Soon he would be in the bedroom demanding to sleep on the bed.

Even with my head under the bedclothes I could still hear the plaintive cry. It began to torment me until I could bear it no longer. At last I sprang out of bed muttering threats and pounded off downstairs to admonish the miserable pup. When I put the light on the crying ceased abruptly. We looked at one another. He wagged his tail, an appendage rather like a rat's. I looked at a pool on the tiles and he looked down at it too, contemplatively, I thought, and then he curled up and settled nose to tail. I put out the light and at once he began to weep. I left the light on and closed the door, telling myself that he could sleep in the light, for one night only, but I had hardly made this concession when he began to cry once more. I stood with my hand on the doorknob trying to decide whether he knew I was there or not. He got out of the box and came and sniffed under the door. I knew it! He was simply trying to get his own way. Well, he wouldn't! I wasn't going to become putty in the hands of a dog! I reached into the room, switched off the light, closed the door and went back up the stairs, half-way at least. He cried. I sat on the stairs and waited for him to give up, but he wouldn't give up and I came down again and hovered outside the door cursing everybody and everything, but quietly, under my breath, and in my mind. The weeping was becoming more than I could stand. Why had I ever allowed the little monster to come across our threshold I wondered?

I looked at my watch. It was five minutes past twelve and I had half hoped to find that it was almost morning. I couldn't stand shivering by the door for the remainder of the night. The thing had become a preposterous affair. I threw back the door, put on the light, picked up the box and the dog with it and brought it out of that. Now I had two other problems. One was to save face. I could hardly return to bed with the pup in a box and admit to my wife that it had made a fool of me. I needed to make up a bed in the back bedroom and keep the dog quiet at the same time. In the morning I would quickly pop him back downstairs into the scullery, and with any luck my wife would never know that I hadn't been by her side throughout the night. How poorly my brain works in the small hours! I fumbled and stumbled, nursing the box in one arm while I hauled and tugged at sheets and blankets. I whispered to the pup to keep quiet, and I must say he obeyed. It seemed to me to be the first indication that he was prepared to do what I wanted, so long as it was what he wanted.

At last I was able to crawl between the sheets and put the box on the floor beside the bed. Jock snuggled up to my hand. With my free hand I pulled the light cord and we were in darkness. I waited until he was asleep and brought my hand into the warmth of the bedclothes. It was a very cold night. Immediately I did this the miserable pup began to weep again. I 'shushed' him to no avail. He didn't know what I meant, and only stopped his crying when I put my hand on him. Once again he snuggled up and seemed to sleep. Once again I lifted my heavy arm back into bed where its circulation might have returned to normal had Jock slept on, but once again he wept. He was missing the contact of other members of the litter. He was lost without the warmth of his brothers and sisters. I should have known, of course, but I couldn't think straight by this time. I was desperate for sleep. I was cold. The bed hadn't been aired. The back bedroom had frost on its window, and the night seemed to be forever. By first light I no longer cared what anyone might think. Jock slept. I slept, with my arm frozen stiff, dangling over the side of the bed. It is surprising how the human body adjusts to pain and discomfort of the most acute kind. Sleep finally overtakes the most wretched of men.

Jock didn't lie abed, of course. His vitality hadn't been in the least diminished by his journey from Cheshire to North Wales. He was out of bed before I opened my eyes, and long before my sleeping left arm could be rubbed back to life. He did his first pool of the day right there by the bed. When my mind finally awoke and got working I knew he would have been just as happy with a hotwater bottle in his box, which was what was done for him the following night when he slept through without weeping, but then I was the sort of young husband who had to learn these things the hard way!

My wife had whispered in my ear that the first-aid for a burst pipe is to tap it with a hammer. She settled Jock in when I had given up laying down the law and made him her dog, completely and utterly. He worshipped her and did anything she asked of him. I suppose, being a terrier he was strong-willed. He could be led, but he couldn't be driven, and above all, he was a woman's dog the way some dogs are men's dogs. The only thing he did for me was to bring up the morning paper when the newsboy delivered it through the letterbox. I am not sure how he came to do this. Perhaps he rushed up and tugged the paper out of the boy's hand as it was being put in the letterbox and I called him. No matter how, he achieved it and he continued to do it, much to my delight, bringing the paper to my bed and delivering it into my hand.

It wasn't long before poor Jock became ill, however. The signs indicated a severe case of distemper, which the vet confirmed with a gloomy shake of his head when he gave the dog his injection. He feared, he said, that there wasn't much hope for him. We had come too late. All we could do was to keep him on the lightest of diets, keep him warm and comfortable and, if he hadn't died in three days, bring him back. I was shocked and horrified at this. I went out and shot some young rabbits which we boiled and fed to the invalid, who now lived in the living room where we had a fire continually burning. The carpet had been taken up and the floor completely covered with newspapers. No human being could have asked for more loving care than my wife gave her wretched little dog. Although he could hardly stand Jock managed to feebly wag his tail when she tended him. He didn't die, and we took him back to the vet in due time. I suppose a mongrel or cross-breed's constitution is much stronger than that of a throughbred but Jock thrived and came back into condition in a short time, his diet sometimes including chicken essence and other delicacies. The only physical effect was a slight stiffness in his back legs which remained with him thereafter.

Jock might have grown to old age with us, but for the fact that soon after his recovery my wife was expecting our child, a daughter, who was born in a nursing home in the village. Jock moped and pined for his mistress and was frantic with delight when she returned. Alas for the poor fellow, he was now no longer the focus of our attention. The nursery was forbidden territory, of course, the fire was screened and a barrier of clothes-horses kept Jock from sitting staring at the red hot coals. He must have felt rejected, I suppose. He displayed none of the usual signs of jealousy, which dogs often do when they are supplanted in a family's affection by the arrival of a child or some new pet. He simply began to wander. He was a stout-hearted, game little dog. He could hold his own with the tattered-eared mongrels of the village and these were his companions whenever he could get out. We fought a losing battle, for all at once he was not to be found. We searched high and low. Villagers nodded their heads and said they had seen a whole string of stray dogs galloping here and there, and one very like Jock among them, but the strays knew nothing of clocks or calendars and went everywhere and anywhere day after day. The village was really no longer a village, except in name, but a sprawling development linked to the town, and Jock vanished for good.

A lost dog is a very sad creature because it is either an unwanted animal or an animal that has run away to escape from a life of misery. Poor Jock left because the light had gone out of his life, I suppose. He ran and ran and was lost among the strays. I liked to think that someone picked him out of the floating population of strays and gave him a good home. We reported his disappearance to the police, and the village policeman, a kindly man, looked diligently for him and refrained from telling us about keeping a dog on a lead and making sure it always had some means of identification on its collar. We never saw Jock again, but we saw his ghost on a hundred occasions—the pennant of his tail, the rough hair of his back, a shaggy face looking at us with bright black eyes. This went on for a number of years. Even now, thirty years afterwards, I sometimes see him, the eternal stray, the lost dog running wild.

I swore we wouldn't have another house dog. There is only one time to bring a dog into the family, and that is when the family is a unit to which a dog may be admitted. The dog may be assimilated, integrated. It has security, which is as important to an animal as it is to a human. If it happens to be of a terrier breed, a pack-hunting dog, it will become the very best kind of family dog. If it is of a larger breed it will almost certainly tend to attach itself to one person and become devoted to that individual in particular. Poor Jock came too early and ran away from the misery of the world. We often talk about him, even yet, for we were to blame.

O.M.H.D.–C

9

A Dog for the Gun

In mitigation of my sins of omission let me say that my wife knew the kind of man I was before I married her. For almost thirty years after that, until I gave up shooting, she was what might be called a shotgun widow. The ways I had acquired were nothing short of an addiction to hunting. I suppose I might have made a shooting dog of Jock, if he had stayed long enough. I might have won him round for hunting is in the blood of all terriers no matter how domesticated they may have become. Without a gundog of my own I would pop down into the village and borrow a poacher's dog to accompany me on my rounds of the farms on which I had permission to shoot. When I wasn't shooting I would borrow a ferret and take the nets. A dog is as important in netting rabbits as in shooting, for he 'marks', that is, he stands and shows by an excited wagging of his tail and his alert attitude that the burrow or warren is tenanted. He trots gaily on past untenanted warrens and gives only the merest sniff at a burrow long disused. Spider was a very rough-haired, ill-proportioned terrier with greying hair. He reminded me of one of the old villagers who had an army haircut and a grey stubble of beard permanently showing on his face. He was a little moth-eaten. His ears were scarred. He had been in many battles and knew the extent of his territory in the village to

a yard, for when he was out in the street he guarded it
against intruders and only when his master took him
ferreting did other dogs dare venture past his door. He
was a little disdainful of me. He looked upon me with a
certain mistrust. I was a foreigner. I didn't speak Welsh
and he was used to being addressed in his native tongue.
'T'yrd one,' his master would say. I said 'Come on,' and it
only served to emphasize that there was something not
quite right about me. He came of course, because an intelligent dog could tell that a knapsack full of nets and the
odour of a ferret in a carrying box meant sport. Off we
would go, up the back road, through the gate, along the
stream and out into the open fields where rabbits ran in
the early morning and late evening. On bright, cold
winter days the odd rabbit might be lying out in a fawn
tuft of grass, but the rest would be snug underground in
the hedge bank, and Spider would give me his verdict on
the potency of the scent. We got on well at this. I would
tell him to sit and wait while I put up the nets and sent the
ferret down to confirm what Spider had shown me by
bolting a rabbit. He was never wrong but he disdained my
praise. He tolerated me and wouldn't stop to be patted. In
fact he growled if I attempted to fondle him at all. It was
as though he wanted to get on with the work and enjoy
the marking of rabbits without being delayed by a lot of
old nonsense from me. He came from a tough household.
Kicks were commoner than caresses and he didn't expect
praise. It was all disconcerting for me for I particularly
liked to 'win' a dog and have it respond. Spider never did.
He was set in his ways and would demonstrate this by
sitting outside the door of the pub at the end of the road
waiting for his master until closing time, no matter how
cold the night. He was a little gone in rheumatism, a little
dull in hearing, and even, I suspected, a little short-
sighted. He was past the age of caring what I thought and
was as independent as a cat.

I remember taking him with the gun. He couldn't

retrieve of course, but he could flush a rabbit, start a hare and once in a while come up on a covey of partridges. On one occasion he came with me on a Saturday afternoon outing that had to be accomplished at a fair pace because I had started late and it would soon be dark. Crossing the first of the dozen or so fields Spider stoppped at a small bush and marked. I looked back at him in annoyance. He was playing the fool because I had almost walked over that bush! I could see through it. I knew there was nothing there. Spider was finally in his second childhood and I was in a hurry. I called him on. He turned his deaf ear. I waved him on, but he couldn't see me. I cursed him and marched on. He sprang into the bush and a fine cock pheasant sailed away—downhill and well out of range of my gun. We looked at each other. I knew what Spider was thinking. If he could have spoken he would have said something blistering about know-alls, and foreigners and people in a hurry. There would have been Welsh swear words mixed up in it and we would have come to blows. All that stopped him was the gun in my hands, I suppose. He found me a rabbit later on, and I shot it before its white dab of cotton wool tail was lost to sight in a gorse clump. Spider wasn't impressed. I put the rabbit in my bag, knowing that he was thinking it should have been a cock pheasant. I suppose he told his master all about it when they stomped their way back from the pub to their little cottage above the stream.

'You know that foreign fellow you let borrow the ferret sometimes? A right Shoni, he is! I marked a cock pheasant for him on Ty Newydd field this afternoon. He walked on! Told me I was a fool. The bloody thing got away!' he would have said. Oh, I knew the way it would be, from the moment the cock pheasant relaxed its wings and dropped its undercarriage to land in the bushes at the bottom of the field. I didn't really like Spider and he had no time for me. The good gundog is a companion, not a hired servant or a borrowed one. A man who shoots with a dog needs to have created a close relationship with the animal. Man and the dog must understand one another, anticipate each other's reaction and act accordingly. You can no more wear another man's boots than shoot with his dog. You must have the right relationship with a gundog.

It was after this that I got my gundog. I never had a lot of initiative in the business of acquiring dogs. Nick's arrival was no exception. My father had a snipe-nosed, South Wales cocker, a rather long-in-the-leg cocker that was inclined to the springer breed. The dog's name was Sherry and she was one of the sort that have it all at birth. She needed next to no training. No one showed her a gun and told her what it was. She already knew. No one told her how far in front she must range. She just did it. She She knew the scent of rabbit and fox, pheasant and partridge, hare and grouse. They came out of her subconscious or at least recognition of them came from there. She must have carried the image of them from a previous existence. My father bred a litter from Sherry and one day he arrived at our door with the second gift dog of our married life. I looked at the offering. It was just over six weeks old. It travelled with its nose to the ground and its ears not yet sweeping the dust on either side of its small, intelligent head. I don't think it bothered to use its eyes at all. Its nose was all it needed. Long afterwards I had ample evidence of this when I could have wished that Nick used his eyes a little more. Well, I said, here was a problem. A gundog must never be turned into a family pet. It should never be mollycoddled but housed in a weatherproof and undraughty kennel, out of doors. It must be fed the right kind of meat and exercised every day according to its kind and its size. I hadn't a kennel. I would have to buy or build one. I would have to rail off an area in which the dog could move about out of the reach of pampering children. I would have to begin as I intended to go on.

The family were used to my laying down the law. They were convinced that the tiny spaniel would overcome my will, and they were almost right, for I found it hard to resist such soulful eyes and that sagacious countenance, rather like a judge in a black wig. I made a kennel, however, and as soon as it was ready out he went to live the spartan life of a gundnog. To tell the truth I almost lived in the kennel myself. I spent every available hour on training, teaching him not to shred the rolled up socks he retrieved for me almost from the first time I asked him to do so. Retrieving and sitting when commanded were his first lessons. Soon, small though he was, I could throw a stuffed rabbit skin in any direction, give a nod, a whistle, or the merest gesture to send him to bring it back to me, or even to stop on command half-way to me with his 'bird' held in his mouth. I didn't need to teach him not to worry his kills for he proved a soft-mouthed dog as soon as his milk teeth were done with. I certainly didn't need to teach him scent. I could take his lead and hurl it away in the dark wherever we were at night and he would cast about and bring it back to me in a few minutes. I could make him sit on an open field and walk away until I was all but hidden from view, sometimes almost a quarter of a mile, before calling him on. He knew my hand signals as well as the whistle. I took him up to the wood and fired a gun over him when he was barely ten weeks old. He knew what it meant.

In those days I was very fond of swimming in the sea and one afternoon I took Nick to the beach with me, leaving him on the shingle while I went in to swim. I had given him no commands. He trotted about, sniffing here and there. I was perhaps a hundred yards out, swimming steadily when I thought I saw a black shadow behind me. I turned and sure enough it was Nick, paddling for all he was worth to keep up and being swung up and down by the waves as he swam. I was deeply touched. He had never been in the water before but of course, like all dogs, he swam instinctively. I turned about and we swam for the shore together. It was a great swim for a small dog that weighed at that time perhaps four or five pounds. I ordered him to sit and await my return while I swam out again. He sat there, looking steadily at me as I went as far out as I usually did, but he waited in vain for my signal to come. I knew that I had only to wave and he would come. I was his lord and master. I think I was his god, and that day the responsibility of being god to anything, even a dog, weighed very heavily upon me.

All the training had but one end, of course, to make Nick my right hand when I went with the gun. I had no intention of asking him to carry an eight or nine pound hare. I relied upon him to flush a rabbit from the hedge, put up a pheasant or track a covey of partridges. People said that it was not wise to ask a dog to retrieve a wood-pigeon until he had been tried in the field and become well-used to picking up game, for the down of a woodpigeon is more than adhesive and will choke an over-eager young dog. I didn't find it so. Nick carried everything I asked him to carry from the start but I remember that day when it all came to fruition. I took my old gamebag and the gun, released Nick from the pen, called him in to my heel, at which he trotted as though tied by a thread, and off we went up the road. He ignored the feeding sheep, the hens in the farmyard, the cats in the barn as I would have expected. He bustled into the hedge when I gave him the signal and bored on at a walking pace until he put out a rabbit. The rabbit bounced away across the field. I swung the gun and brought it down at maximum range. Nick peered out of the underbrush, his head draped in grasses and sticky-willie. I gave him the signal. He jumped clear of the tangles and quickly galloped out to bring back the rabbit, holding it firmly, gently and squarely in his mouth. He delivered it as he had delivered the dummy, putting his forefeet on my bent knee. I took it from him and put it into my bag. I watched him go back into the hedge and moved on after him. I was delighted. He knew the name of the game from that day on, although on this occasion he didn't make a great bag. Later in the day I saw partridges come out of a root field and sail down in a neat arc to drop into the clover, a move partridges make at set times in the day. I took Nick with me and it wasn't long before he picked the scent and followed it where the breeze had wafted it, looking like that long-ago advertisement for the Bisto kids as he traced the source. Soon after the tail end of the covey rose and I shot one of them. The bird fell out of sight in a hazel thicket. Nick was soon in the thicket and came back under a wire fence with the partridge in his mouth. That was enough. The covey had run on by this time, and we let them go because they had everything in their favour, a great clump of hazels and broom along a gully, places where Nick could track them, but I couldn't hope to follow and shoot. We came home very tired and happy. We had achieved what we had set out to achieve.

10

Give a Dog a Good Home

THE fascination of having a dog that understood my every gesture and even anticipated what I was going to do remained undiminished. I knew that he watched me all the time. I never had to remind him that we were turning off to the left or right or, if I climbed over some obstacle such as a fence of sagging barbed wire which he wouldn't be able to crawl under or jump over, where I was heading. He always seemed to sense the direction and he knew where we would meet if he had to make a detour and he made his detour and waited for me. He didn't wag his tail and ask for praise. He was much too intelligent for that. His efficiency was built-in. He didn't look at me with scorn if I missed anything but on the other hand I believed him when he told me there was a rabbit or a pheasant in a bush. We followed scents together from gorse clump to gorse clump, along a stream, across a bank, into the wood. He travelled nose down with his black stump of a tail gently wagging. The wagging would increase, becoming faster when the scent was strengthening. It diminished accordingly when he found that his quarry was long gone. He could pick up the trail of a rabbit or a hare and show me its route as a matter of interest, but when I went with serious intention he never seemed to dally over old scents. There are gundogs that are fussers and loiterers about the bushes, absent-minded creatures that get absorbed in scents, not only of game, but of small things like field mice. There are dogs that don't know a duck from a waterhen because they have never seen the former put in the bag and the latter allowed to scuttle off along the side of the brook. Such dogs are usually absent-minded and uneducated. Their owners become too respectful of the dog at work, or seeming to be at work, and allow him to hang about like a schoolboy playing truant. Nick didn't make this mistake about scents and I never had to remind him what the game was. We had little demonstrations for our mutual benefit. I would carry a large smooth pebble and toss it into a hayfield, having sent Nick off up the road and made him sit while I threw the stone. I would know where it had fallen, but he wouldn't, and I would signal him to come back to me and go and seek the stone. In this way I could watch him working the ground upwind, finding the scent and tracing it. Scent drifts like the smoke from a chimney and Nick's path to the pebble was like a contour map. He never cut corners or used his eyes if the stone happened to be lying on short grass and visible to both of us. I was happy enough at this although more demanding dog-trainers might have expected their charges to lift their heads and use their eyes. Often when I shot something Nick would follow scent and I would discover that it was the best way because the bird had fallen but hadn't been too badly shot and was able to slip off into cover. About the only time he turned a deaf ear to my calling him off was when he was on the trail of a wounded bird or a rabbit I had decided I had missed but had actually wounded.

Our excursions together were weekly but I exercised him every day, rain hail or shine. We walked something like six miles at a brisk pace and on the quiet back roads would go through our drill. I would drop the leash or a glove and we would walk on. After going perhaps two hundred yards I would tell him I had dropped the leash and he was to go back and get it. I would say this to him in a conversational tone, as my grandfather had done to his dog. Nick would about turn and go lolloping down the road to find the leash. When I judged he was nearly upon it I would turn round and whistle him to sit and he would sit until I told him to retrieve. I would put up my hand or whistle him to sit again, sometimes three or four times before he rejoined me. Occasionally he seemed to know that I had dropped the leash or glove and would look up at me as we plodded along but he never went back unless ordered to do so. Now and again I deliberately tried to disconcert him by ordering him over the hedge and out into the field instead of back along the road. I would make him sit there and then tell him to go and find the leash. He would either come back onto the road directly or cut diagonally across the field and emerge somewhere within range of the thing I had dropped. He never broke the rules and I am sure he loved the game.

On some occasions I took him across the rough pasture above the village where we would pass through flocks of grazing sheep. He never as much as looked in the direction of the sheep and when I met the farmer unexpectedly one day and quickly assured him that Nick was a completely obedient dog he grinned and said he had been watching us for a long time. The dog was the most obedient creature he had ever seen. He had been amazed at the way Nick could be signalled to clap down, sit up, make a detour or wait for me by the slightest of hand movements. Nick sat on his haunches while the farmer was saying this. His eyes never left my face. He simply waited for me to have done talking. He would have waited until nightfall, as steady as one of the china dogs my grandmother used to keep on the parlour mantelpiece. It was our outings across the sheep grazings that almost cost poor Nick his life, however. All at once he began to look so glossy coated that I might have known something was wrong. He became leaner than usual and I at last came to the conclusion that he had worms. I had wormed him as a pup

but somehow he had become reinfected with these parasites. I bought the usual proprietary remedies but they did
nothing. I grated agar nut but this did nothing either. I
took him to the vet and the vet shook his head and said he
had tapeworm from the sheep grazings, something more
dangerous than the sheep tick which can attach itself to a
dog's underbelly and cause pain and serious injury. He
gave me a prescription and I took it home and doctored
poor Nick. The net result was nothing. When a tape
worm really takes hold it needs something like a depth
charge to dislodge it. The stronger the dog and the more
serious the infestation the harder it is to dislodge the para-
site because the dog must be almost poisoned himself
before the wretched worm gives up its hold. Nick became
leaner and more ravenous. I became more depressed and
went back to the vet for his ultimate weapon, an oily con-
coction which he said the dog would have to be forced to
swallow. I had to manhandle the poor fellow to get his
dose down him. It was no use telling him that it was all
for his own good. He knew only his hunger and he had
never seen a tapeworm. For a day he stood listlessly looking at the wire of his pen and then all at once he evacuated
his parasites, five of them, one almost eighteen inches in
length and almost half an inch in width. The tapeworm is
well named?

After this serious setback, due mainly to my lack of
knowledge of the subject and my slow realization that
something was seriously wrong, Nick had to be brought
back into condition and his stamina improved. I fed him
bones, liver, green vegetables, good meat and vitamins,
and he recovered, much to everyone's relief and delight,
for although he was a gundog and not a family pet the
family loved him and continually pleaded for him to be
given his freedom. He wasn't housetrained, however. He
had spent his formative dog years learning other things
than nice manners. He didn't know what chairs and
carpets were about. If I happened to open the pen and go

back indoors to collect my gun and bag he would dash round the room and barge under tables and chairs as though on the scent of a rabbit. It was the only time excitement really got the better of him.

When I look back at it all now I think I should have done something about Nick before we came to the awful moment when we had to part. We had lived in the house for a number of years as tenants but when first one of the old ladies who owned the property became ill and then died and the second was afflicted with some serious illness we were given the option of buying and did so despite the fact that a great deal needed to be done to put the place in order. One of the first things was the taking down of a small conservatory at the back and the digging out of the yard below the steeply rising garden. The difficulty here was that this work would be a major operation and the builder needed considerable time to hack out the old asphalt, re-level the drain covers etc. before he could lay a new surface. Nick's kennel would simply have to be taken to bits. There was no room for it in the garden above. We had hardly embarked upon our transaction to put things right before I was compelled to face the fact that Nick couldn't remain with us, but is it right to give a dog away? Is it right to leave it with anyone like a piece of left luggage and then have it back again? Time to a dog is happiness or desolation. It doesn't know the month, the day or even the hour, and it is no use telling it that the morning will soon come or we will meet again in a month. I wrestled with my conscience while the builder began to arrange his schedules, fixing up the men, the tools and the materials he would need to re-do the yard, take out a scullery or larder window, replaster walls and so on. I couldn't sell Nick as a trained gundog. I would give him to someone who could provide him with a kennel out of doors and exercise him in the way in which he had been brought up. Nick loved company. He was always excited when children were around. Although he was a gundog and a very mature one he was still a pup at heart and a very lovable dog. I couldn't bear to look him in the face because I felt he would read my mind. At last I met a man who said he would be delighted to have him. His family loved animals. I warned him that poor Nick just didn't know what a kitchen was. He was absolutely untrained and a madman indoors, but Nick's friendliness was touching. He was irresistible. His tail wagged nineteen to the dozen. He shimmied with delight and almost shook the long black ears from his head. At least he would be in the hands of people who really loved dogs and knew what a dog's life should be.

The parting so far as I was concerned was painful but Nick sprang into his collar and was away, bustling out of the gate, leaving his kennel in the yard and only once looking back to see if I had some order to give. I didn't raise my hand. I looked at him, aware that he lived for the moment. There was no tomorrow. What he remembered of yesterday I couldn't really tell. His instinct had made him easy to train. He didn't dally on old scents. Life was here and now. I consoled myself with these thoughts as he lumbered away down the road, eager to see where he was being taken, to smell new smells and meet new people. I looked at the empty kennel and felt very depressed. That evening the builder, who was also a jobbing plumber, came up to do some small job and said he would need to have the yard cleared as soon as possible. Our job was next on the list and it would take a fair bit of his time. Materials were hard to get and unless he could put them to use he might not get his next order filled quite as quickly. I went out and began taking down the run, dismantling the kennel. I had time. Nick wasn't there for the six mile walk and the training ritual. It was summer and I wouldn't be shooting until autumn. I tried not to think about it, but underneath it all I knew I had come close to betraying my dog, delivering him into the hands of the philistines and taking the easy way out. A dog isn't something that can be sold or given away. It should never be taken in in the first place unless the intention is to give it a dog's life and to respect it as a member of the family.

A lot of my enthusiasm for shooting waned after Nick departed. I didn't see him again. I had reports of him. The change seemed to have done him no harm. He was happy and comfortable though wilder in his ways than an ordinary domesticated dog. He simply wouldn't be house-trained and on wet days he would bundle in with his new family, shaking his coat and leaving great splodgy footprints and trails of water everywhere he went. He was a very lovable creature, they said, and full of life. He hadn't moped or pined. I felt a little better at this news, but nevertheless had a strong sense of guilt about having abandoned him. I would never take on a dog again unless I could be sure that I would stand by it through thick and thin. A dog may be given away but responsibility for it can't. In the end poor Nick was moved on once more, this time to a farm where he was fussed over and permitted to lie steaming before the fire, his muddy footprints ignored. But I never felt happy about having given him away in the first place.

II

The Wanderer

My father had been thinking of retiring for some time
when he came across an advertisement for the cottage and
land which he asked me to view for him before going
further. I went and looked over the place. It was tucked
away at the end of a rough lane, three or four hundred
yards from the nearest neighbour in any direction. It was
screened by trees and the property included a long vinery,
a very long greenhouse and a single greenhouse. All of
these with heating installation fallen into disrepair and not
fit to work again. I loved the secret garden, the old orchard,
the sundial on the way up to the pine wood. I was delighted
with the slate courtyard and the old stone potting shed and
sent back a glowing report to Father who came down to see
for himself. Before very long he had arranged to buy the
place. Now, of course, he had to face up to retirement and
he really wasn't ready to make the decision. The cottage
had to be looked after. I went over every week and Mother
and Father came down at week-ends, for they had sent on
enough furniture to make the place habitable. Five years
passed before Father came to the decision to have done
with engineering and the manufacture of things like
broaching machines and injection moulding equipment.
It was a big step from the world of engineering schedules
and the design office to keeping hens and tending bees.

Father threw himself at everything. He was like an ant trying to move a mountain. He worked harder than he had ever done. He dug and delved, cultivated, weeded, tore things down and rebuilt them nearer to his heart's desire. He constructed henruns, converted an outsized kennel in which the former owner of the cottage had kept a huge St Bernard into a chicken house, and did the same to a summer-house which had been tucked away in the trees but was now brought down and established on the edge of the kitchen garden. The farmer in Father tended to awaken every so often and he not only increased his flock of laying hens with a variety of point-of-lay pullets but added ducks and geese, khaki campbell ducks and Emden and Toulouse geese. He began to build a garage of limestone, using the entrance to the kitchen garden where two walls about six feet high flanked the road. It never struck him that he wouldn't live forever. He made work for himself. It all would be beyond his strength by the time he had finished his henruns, rosebeds and the like. I suppose he was obsessed with a fear that if he didn't work he would be an old man. He had always had contempt for people who sat back and made the excuse that they had earned their rest, or the world owed them a living.

Mother did her best to keep up, but she had had heart trouble and her heart condition wasn't improving. In fact she was becoming increasingly short of breath and unable to do her own self-appointed tasks. In a short time the doctor ordered her into a nursing home. Father became his own cook and bottle washer, dashing to the nursing home to visit her every day and taking little offerings from the garden, flowers, fruit and so on. Alas she was hardly able to appreciate how manfully he was coping. She fretted to get home and at last the doctor agreed. Mother had been home only a few weeks however before a more serious attack laid her low. She was rushed into hospital but a week or so later she died. The dream of retirement had come to nothing. Father was shocked. He had refused to believe that this might happen. He was on his own and he could think of nothing better to do than go on working at his garden projects, slashing nettles, weeding the vinery, building the garage that would stand a direct hit from one of the Lancasters he had built during the war. The days were short and the nights were long. If the telephone happened to ring he was startled. He refused to give up. He had his livestock to look after. He couldn't go away, he said. He brooded and tried to hide the fact that he was desperately lonely. The first indication of his loneliness was when he arranged to buy a cairn puppy. Rory came from Wester Ross. He had been bred by a Mrs Mackenzie who farmed up there, and he had a fine pedigree. I wasn't told that he was on his way and knew nothing about the transaction until I called and was greeted by father with the pup in the crook of his arm.

'This is Rory', he said. Rory looked at me with bright little black eyes. He and father were both small and wiry. They both bristled. Rory's beard was just growing. It was dark grey. He was full of vitality. Nothing could daunt him. Father told me how intelligent his dog was, how knowing, how affectionate. He didn't say that he was completely untrained and prone to making pools on the carpet without warning, but then most puppies are. They come untrained and have to be taught civilized behaviour. I had a feeling that Father had too much on his hands to undertake Rory's domestic training. Rory trotted at his heels wherever he went and might have been tied to his foot by a length of string. They went shopping together in the old Austin which Father wouldn't part with because he had driven so many thousands of miles in it before the war and had taken his father to so many places in it. Rory occupied Mother's seat and sat on his haunches looking from left to right, enjoying every minute of the journey. They went to the corn depot and into town. They went visiting. Rory was never parted from his master. It was a case of love me, love my dog. Where Rory wasn't welcome, and it can be something of a nuisance to discover that a dog hasn't been house-trained, Father wouldn't go. He had Rory sitting at the table with him when he took his meals. Rory shared his armchair, tucked down between his master and the arm of the chair. He also slept on his master's bed. They worshipped one another and forgave one another for sins committed as well as sins of omission. The lady in Wester Ross was written to and told what a wonderful companion she had provided and what an intelligent little fellow Rory had turned out to be. Rory lapped it all up. He was in heaven, treated like the prodigal son, fed like a prince. It was all sad and almost pathetic.

Father was not really a great engineer in the kitchen. He could boil water and make tea. He could scramble an egg, but he tended to leave a stew boiling on the cooker and go off to work in the garden with Rory for company and return only when he or Rory felt the pangs of hunger. By this time the pot would have boiled dry, the stew would have become a charred mass and the ceiling darkened like the inside of a kippering shed. More than once he had to devote a day to cleaning up the disastrous mess. More than once both he and Rory had to make do with improvised meals. They decided that a housekeeper would have to be found. Poor Rory couldn't have had second sight, or he would never have agreed, for the housekeeper's arrival was the beginning of the end of his happiness. Almost the day after the lady was installed Father was taken ill and rushed to hospital where he was operated upon in a matter of hours. Rory was cut off from the master he worshipped. His whole world had darkened. To make matters worse, he wasn't allowed to have the run of the house. He couldn't sleep on his master's bed. He was scolded and rushed out of doors when he forgot his manners. He no longer sat at the table enjoying a one-sided conversation about plans for the day. The sun had gone down and he was inconsolable. There was nothing else for him to do but run away.

Father's stay in hospital proved to be a long one. He was kept there for seventeen weeks or more. He was visited every day by members of the family and his house-keeper, who at first kept from him the news that Rory had gone walk-about. Rory was found before too long. The police and everyone for miles around became familiar with that small, black-faced, wandering dog, for he would hardly be restored to his own territory before he was off again. I often thought about poor Jock and the way he had run off. Father was told by one of his visitors that Rory had been found that particular afternoon. This was his first intimation that his beloved dog was wandering and he demanded an explanation. Rory must be brought to the hospital so that he could see him! He wouldn't believe that he was being looked after. And so Rory was brought to the hospital grounds. Someone carried him along the windows of the ward in which his master lay. Father raised himself on his elbow, weak and emaciated though he had become, and looked at the whiskered face of Rory pressed against the window. Rory whined and cried and wagged his tail. Father, who was pitifully weak, wiped a tear from his cheek. Rory was taken home but immediately went missing again. Perhaps he was doing his best to locate the hospital, or perhaps, like father, he was trying to lose himself.

At the end of his long period of hospitalization Father was reunited with Rory. By this time Rory had learned to cock his leg on items of furniture to show his contempt for the good lady who looked after the house. He regarded her as an intruder in what had been a perfect world, and he behaved badly. For his master he had nothing but adoration. He squealed with hysterical delight when they met, nuzzling his hand, trying to get as close to him as he could, watching him with excitement and never taking his eyes from him. Father was choked with emotion. They had come through a bad time together. Rory meant a great deal to him, so much that he insisted that he be allowed to sleep on his bed as before and share his armchair no matter how often he left wet patches on the lounge carpet. This didn't stop Rory wandering, however. Perhaps it was because he wasn't given the front seat in the car when the shopping was done or it may simply have been that he felt he had been displaced, rejected. He never regained the spirit and sparkle he had had before Father's illness. Their days together wouldn't be long, although Rory would live to be more than seventeen years old.

It was during his recuperation that Father began to express the conviction that every family should include a dog. A dog was not just man's best friend. He was a companion, loyal, faithful, affectionate! Children should always be brought up with a dog. It taught them to respect and love animals. A dog was company for a woman in the house. A dog would give warning of intruders. There was nothing a dog couldn't do, it seemed. Most of this campaign was directed to our taking a dog into the family. It was selfish of me to refuse my wife and children the delight of having a dog! Whether I liked it or not the children were going to have a dog and the dog was ordered. It would be from the same kennel as Rory had come from. It would be a bitch because bitches were more trustworthy with children. I didn't know what to say. Father was a very sick man. I knew it, but he was blissfully unaware of the fact. I could hardly discourage him. Rory had given him so much pleasure. He was convinced that a dog meant happiness and to live without one was no life at all. We talked about it. The children, of course, wanted a dog. Most children do. My wife had been fascinated by the black-bearded face of Rory and his endearing puppy behaviour, although she had been a little less than fascinated by his habits indoors!

We were due to go on holiday and Father too, had been persuaded to take a fortnight by the sea at the other end of the county, although his doctor had said the sea in one place was very much the same as the sea forty miles along the coast. We wrote to Mrs Mackenzie in Wester Ross, explaining our difficulty. Father had jumped the gun. We would be ready to have the dog which had been reserved for us, if she would only keep it for a few weeks more while we went to our rented cottage in South Caernarvonshire. Dear me, we said, Father was determined to make us have a dog. He was quite obsessed with the idea and there was no way out of it.

I little knew that this would be the dog of my life. I would be completely taken over by that dog as Father had been by Rory. She would become as important to me as my own children. Every member of the family would look upon her as one of us. I said the dog might come. The children could make a pet of it, but I really didn't want a dog in the house. If I had another dog it would be a gun-dog. I would have nothing to do with this one but I wouldn't disappoint Father. I couldn't daunt his spirit when he so plainly didn't have long to live.

12

Susy's Journey

NOWHERE in Britain can properly be called remote any more for the most distant corner of the country may be reached in a matter of hours by plane, or even by car if one has the endurance to drive. Wester Ross has no direct link with North Wales, however. In the sense that it takes a good part of the day to come out of the Western Highlands by train to reach Glasgow and change trains for the South, Wester Ross might have been more than remote to a miserable pup nailed up in a tea-chest. Wales, if she could have had any conception of the place to which she was being forwarded, would have been the uttermost end of the earth. Susy, of course, could have no understanding of what was happening to her at all. She lay curled up in the few handfuls of hay that had been laid for her to rest upon and suffered the rattling and swaying of the train as it wound its way out of the mountains and rumbled on to Glasgow. She did what even man must do when there is no relief for his discomfort, and put up with it although it must have seemed forever. In Glasgow perhaps some porter read the message on the crate and gave poor Susy a drink, for Mrs Mackenzie had carefully painted these words on the tea-chest. If he did I doubt very much whether Susy was able to lift her head and lap the water. Her nightmare went on for a day and a night and almost another day. I suppose it could have been no less for her half-brother, Rory, but I wasn't at the cottage to see Rory at the end of his ordeal.

Susy's arrival had been awaited all day with rising excite-ment among the children. The station had been telephoned half a dozen times, but the porters had no dogs to report. The man in the parcels office pondered the distance to Wester Ross. 'Must be 'undreds of miles,' he told me when I telephoned. 'It's up in the north of Scotland, you see.' After he had sensed that I was waiting for something more he added that he had 'never had nothing' from there. Following a timetable of trains through places like Glasgow and Carlisle, to say nothing of Stirling, when I couldn't say when the dog had been sent off would be too much. The dog would have to change trains, you see, maybe more than once, but have no fear, it would be marked livestock, and livestock was never neglected.

At home that afternoon the children waited for the next down train and rang the station again while Susy's ordeal continued, hour after hour of it, a sort of hell inflicted on a small animal which until that day had known only the deep silence of the glen and the cry of the curlew. When at last I was told that 'ewer little dog is 'ere' I discovered that my daughter had already obtained this information. Without waiting for me to take her to the station he had dashed down and gone there on the bus. I got in the car and followed, knowing that they would have to be brought back, but by the time I reached the station all that re-mained there was the crate. The dog had been snatched out of it, comforted and carried off to make the final stage of her long journey by bus. I managed to get the tea-chest into the boot of the car and tied the lid down with string. The man in the parcels department shook his head. Such a lot of fuss about a dog not much bigger than a man's boot! He had expected a Great Dane, I suppose, or a St Bernard with the brandy barrel hanging from its neck. The tea-chest was big enough, anyway. I drove off feeling that it wasn't my day at all. When I got home it certainly wasn't. No one had time to hear my story. No one had time to look up from the little dog lying exhausted and asleep on an old dressing-gown spread in front of the fire. It was a touching sight. I counted the heads of my children and realized that half the children of the village were involved in this, as well as my own family. The little blond dog didn't move. She breathed and that was all. She was six hundred miles from home and the awful rattling, and the thunder of bogeys lurching and swaying over points, was at an end. Nothing is forever though it may seem to be! The circle of worshippers had to be broken up so that I could have my tea. Things had got a little out of perspective, I said. A dog is a dog and they are all lovable little creatures when they are pups, but a sense of proportion must be preserved. Susy had travelled a long, long way, but she was alive. She would soon get on her feet and start making a great nuisance of herself. Like Rory, she would make pools on the carpet. She wasn't like Rory, they said. She was blond and neat and she smiled! I couldn't believe the smile until I bent over and looked at the pup. She wasn't smiling. She had an undershot jaw and her little milk teeth protruding from her lips seemed to suggest that she was smiling. I couldn't help admitting that she looked a most attractive little thing, lying there sleeping the sleep of the dead.

There would be rules for Susy like anyone else in the family, I said. She would conform. She wouldn't be like Rory who had had his own way for far too long. No, things would start as they would go on. She would be the children's pet. She would be house-trained. I would have nothing to do with her. There were frowns of disapproval at my pronouncements. No one could be hard-hearted towards such a delightful little animal! I looked at Susy and wondered about it all. No, a household couldn't be allowed to revolve around anything so small and insignificant. It was absurd to allow it to happen. It wasn't going to happen, do you hear? Susy awoke and looked at each one of us. She was able to get on her feet and wobble across the floor to introduce herself, her tail wagging. I suppose man's first step towards being civilized, and he still has a thousand miles to go, was when he was touched by the helplessness of the weak and the young and felt compelled to protect them. The maternal instinct isn't entirely and strictly in accordance with a state of civilization, for it can be ruthless and quite brutal, but savage man became something a little better than a beast when he held out his hand in compassion and helped the helpless. I wasn't ashamed to find that the small dog did something to my emotions and somehow took away my mind. I couldn't help myself. What is a sentimentalist but a person with compassion for the helpless? Is there anything to be ashamed of in that?

The children adored the little dog. The little dog had found a litter, affection, and warmth. The world was perfect. She took a drink and had some food and went off to sleep. It is wonderful the way a dog accepts human beings in place of its own kind, and how it integrates with the family group without anyone having to persuade it to do so. Susy did this from the moment she was taken in. She was lavished with care and attention. Friends of the children came to the back door to see her. There was never a dull moment. Everyone wanted to stroke her puppy coat which would grow long and soft and sleek. Everyone smiled to see her smile and ooh-ed and ah-ed when she toddled up to them wagging her tail There is nothing like a pup to win people over! The petshop owner sits like a spider in a web knowing that the bait is out if he has one pot-bellied mongrel pup sleeping in his shop window. The world will gather there and people will come in and buy whether they want to or not. I suppose Father had known that Susy would be irresistible and we would be in raptures about her from the moment we set eyes upon her, but although I admit I was mesmerized and completely taken over, I never realized the extent to which this small dog would influence my life! There would be few people with whom we would leave her. She would be the focus of our existence as a family, no matter what outsiders thought or how much they raised their eyes to heaven and smiled!

Father agreed that she was a wonderful little dog but not, of course, quite so wonderful as his own. I had to admit that Rory had a pedigree and Mrs Mackenzie hadn't bothered to send one for Susy. Susy was quite plainly not a show dog. She would never win at Crufts and wouldn't be looked at twice at the local dog show. Her undershot jaw suggested that she had been the runt of her litter. She was otherwise sound in wind and limb, however, and full of high spirits. She was a most gentle little animal, never in the least vicious and, unlike Rory, she needed very little training. She was a naturally clean, fastidious little dog and from the start it was obvious that she would fit into the family. The one thing she couldn't stand was noise. She hated the sound of trains or anything that sounded at all like a train and would cringe or shrink from the sound. She was a poor traveller. The car made her sick and I suppose the sound and vibration of its locomotion reminded her of that awful journey from Wester Ross. We had to give her a pill in order to take her the six or seven miles from our house to the cottage and this of course left her limp and lethargic for most of the time she was there. She needed a sedative to let her go home again. It was all too much to inflict on a pup and we began to organize our outings to suit Susy. We didn't leave her by herself in the house. We were concerned for her happiness and her comfort, even at this stage in her life.

A dog in the family rounds it off, dog-lovers will tell you. This is true. People can't quarrel with a dog though they may bicker with one another. They may be mean to one another but they can't be mean to a helpless dog with soulful, worshipping eyes. Children who can be quite greedy and selfish will share their food with a puppy and show concern for the dog's well-being. In a short time we all became involved with Susy. When one of us had been out or away for a time the first question they would ask would be 'Where is Susy? How is she?' Susy would come trundling out from under the table or jump down from the bed we had bought her to greet the newcomer. Her welcome was heart-warming and quite touching. It would always be so, even when she was an old dog in her sixteenth year when getting about wasn't particularly easy and her energy was flagging. The children vied with one another to take her for walks and she was a pup among pups, as happy as a dog could ever be.

Alas for poor Rory, his life was to be less idyllic. Father's health was deteriorating. He was becoming concerned about himself as he had never been before. Perhaps he had some premonition of his end but even so he did his best to complete the garage he had been building. He put the old car on one side as a relic and got himself a new one. Rory still went everywhere with him, of course. Rory worshipped him and would until the end. The end was not far away. Father telephoned us to wish us a happy New Year and I knew from his voice that he was far from well. Not long afterwards he asked me to drive him to hospital where his doctor had arranged a bed for him. In less than a fortnight he was dead and Rory was a lost dog without running away. He looked for his master. When he looked at me I think he knew that he was dead. I never again saw him look as he had done when they had been constant companions. What could we do about him now? We had Susy and there might have been a chance that they would have got on together as part of the same family. They were both sensitive terriers however and the danger was that one or the other would suffer. Father had never thought that he would die and leave Rory, although he had talked about death and his affairs in general. At the funeral we talked about the dog and one of my younger brothers said that he would take Rory into his family. There was nothing else for it. Rory would be happy with children. He would forget his misery. Even human beings forget or overcome their grief to a degree.

Rory was taken off to live in Cheshire. He was happy in his new home and as well loved as he had ever been, but he never got rid of the wandering habit he had developed when Father went to hospital for the first time. He came back to the cottage several times. I think he remembered his puppyhood for he seemed to be delighted to be here. He lived to be even older than Susy and died when he was in his eighteenth year. Father would have been in his eighty-fifth year had he lived. I am sure he thought he and Rory wouldn't die, but would go on forever, which is the way a man should face life anyhow. Time is meaningless to a dog. Although people are fond of saying that time is money it is a commodity money can't buy. For a man as well as a dog living is now, and time is a deathly conception of life!

13

Removal

WE had all come to stay at the cottage in the last few days of Father's life. Now we went home again, leaving his housekeeper to look after the place while we sorted out our affairs and prepared to come for a longer stay until it was decided what to do about the property. There was some to-ing and fro-ing and we finally settled down at the cottage for four months. It suited the children. They had freedom they had only rarely enjoyed. They could wander where they liked within our boundary, light a fire and play at cooking meals. The hens had all gone. So had the ducks and the geese. The Bank, who were Father's executors, decided that the livestock should be sold and I wasn't sorry for I had enough to do. I was busily occupied writing a weekly piece for two national magazines and I had a novel to write for my publisher. At the same time I was secretary of an engineering company, a job I found increasingly irksome and time-consuming. Every day on my way to the office I would drop the children off at the grammar school. There would be a decision to be made about schools if we decided to sell our old house and move. In all this family upheaval, and there was much more upheaval than the foregoing may suggest, Susy was content just to be with us. Everything we did was new and exciting and she was in everything, swarming over us and getting under our feet. She was never chided for this. We regarded her as another child in the family and we were beginning to consider things with reservation about whether Susy would like it or not, or whether we could inflict this or that upon her. Outsiders would have raised their eyebrows and scorned our concern for a small, insignificant dog. A Great Dane would have been an encumbrance almost anyone, dog-lover or not, would have had to consider, but a small dog, not yet a year old! Only rarely was I able to come down to earth and wonder if we weren't becoming eccentrics. Our first consideration was would the dog be happy, would she like what we were thinking of doing? We had other high priorities. Would she enjoy liver or some fresh meat from the butcher, or perhaps today she would like some lamb's hearts! Was she comfortable in her bed? The kitchen was a bit remote from the bedroom and she would be miserable in the night! I suppose without being aware of it we even weighed up whether the cottage was the right place to bring her, but there wasn't really much doubt of that. Susy loved the place. Where our old, steep back garden had been measured in square yards here we had acres in which a small dog could roam.

The problem of whether we should take over the cottage and sell our house was complicated by the fact that it was part of my father's estate and the bank, as banks always seem to do, were determined to justify their existence and take forever settling the estate. God save us all from the banks. They are good at looking after money and so reluctant to part with it that one often wonders who earned it in the first place! This is by the way. We did seriously debate the move because my wife had never been used to living in complete isolation. She would be alone for a good part of each day with only our infant son and the dog for company. While this might have been no great ordeal for someone who had lived on a farm or in the wilds somewhere it was a serious consideration. It wasn't that we needed neighbours so much as we needed the reassurance of having them within hailing distance and our neighbours were far out of earshot! There was always little Susy, of course. She had already established her territory and barked when anyone passed or came within yards of the house. She simply bounced with indignation when someone called and I often thought how irritating the barking must have been to people passing quietly along the footpath that flanks the lane. No matter, the die was cast. Our debating came to an end. We decided to take the cottage and move. It was, after all, an ideal place for a writer to do his work. It was as peaceful as any place I had ever lived in, and completely secluded. With Susy to warn her of the approach of callers my wife felt she could put up with it. It would be a long time before she became conditioned to this kind of life but she would, and finally she would want privacy and seclusion above anything else, something that very few people can hope for in this crowded modern world.

The removal could only take place after we had disposed of Father's furniture and other effects, sold our old house and decided what we wanted doing to the cottage before we took over. We had lived a long time in that old house. It was the background to our married life. We had improved it as far as we were able. We had raised a family there and kept two dogs there. The children had loved the village and all their friends would be left behind. Some people move every few years, even every few months of their lives, and are used to the upheaval, but moving house proved a traumatic experience for us. It does for a great many people who ask no more of life than to be allowed to put down roots and stay put. It is different with a dog. A dog's happiness seems to depend not so much on place as familiar objects and being within the family or the litter. It will cheerfully move on. Possessions are of no significance so long as it sleeps in its own bed or wrapped in its own blanket. Thoreau's utilitarian, frugal existence would have been perfect with a dog for company but I don't recall a dog in Walden. The day came when we saw the last of our furniture packed for removal to the cottage. Susy's bed, which had been to and fro several times, went too. We moved in on a bright, sunny Saturday and treated ourselves to a bottle of champagne to warm the house. Susy dug for a mouse on the slope above the court but didn't manage to get it. The hole is there yet.

We still had a thousand things to do. The grass in the old orchard had grown knee-high. The kitchen garden was like a concentration camp with its perimeter of poles and wire, its coops and huts. The old vinery had shed a few panes of glass. The greenhouses needed straightening and indoors everything seemed to need moving round and trying in new places. We had had the solid fuel cooker taken out and replaced with a hot water boiler for the radiators. The boiler suffered from internal rumblings and Susy was very nervous of it. I felt that anthracite fumes might affect her and wondered whether she should be allowed to sleep in the living-room. Susy had already decided where she was going to sleep, come what might, one day. She was going to share our bedroom and nothing was going to stand in her way, if it took her a dog's life-time to get there!

I don't think there was a day when Susy's beard wasn't stuck up with the debris of dead leaves or pine needles. She was always rooting in the bushes, always scratching and digging because she was a hunting dog. She loved being out of doors and only came in to assure herself that we hadn't left her. She barked in the bushes and told us that she was busy and we always knew roughly where she was. 'Supper Sue!' someone would call and she would emerge from the great forest of green periwinkle, her little head cocked as though she tipped her small brain into one corner in order to concentrate on the meaning of the summons. 'Isn't she a lovely dog?' we would ask one another. The word lovely became particularly significant. I think she began to consider it part of her name.

My habit of aping the arabs and never standing where I could sit and never sitting where I could lie delighted Susy from puppyhood onwards. She loved to discover me in a reclining position. Her philosophy was never to let a sleeping man lie without lying down herself—outstretched on his abdomen and stomach, and looking into his face. She loved to do this. Sometimes out of sheer mischief she would stand up and study my face closely, making little sounds to encourage me to open an eye. If I failed to respond she would touch me with her cold, wet nose and I had to let her see that I was awake, whereupon she would wag her tail frantically and I would fondle her head. It was all a sort of mutual reassurance that we still loved one another, for when I had given her a gentle pat or two she would settle down and sleep as only a dog can. Sometimes she would dream and chase a mouse through the grass with little excited yelps and whimpers and I would open my eyes and watch her, knowing that she was more than a body but a dog spirit, a dreamer of dog dreams, just as I was a dreamer. There was always some kind of subconscious fear that the spirit would be disembodied and I could never resist the temptation to touch her and tell her that she was all right. I was never comfortable when my children talked in their sleep as they sometimes did but I can't say why. Susy would awaken and to all appearances her dream would be completely out of her mind. I don't think she remembered them as humans remember dreams. Once again she seemed to tell me that life is now, not yesterday and not tomorrow, and when I dislodged her she would assume that we had something more important to do than lie on the settee dreaming and taking our ease. We had. We had a million things to do, things to dismantle and tidy up, changes to make, to say nothing of cutting back the jungle that encroached with every summer day that passed. It was the jungle that delighted Susy more than anything else. She bored into it like a miniature buffalo or bison. Tunnelling through bushes, thorns and the en-

tanglements of blackberry and bracken came second nature
to Susy. It was a game of which she never tired from
puppyhood to old age. Her progress would be marked by
a swaying of stems and stalks and she sometimes gave a
little yelp of pain as she was brought up short by a long
thorn but she never turned back. Whatever it was she
trailed or tracked she never came up with it, but the excitement was the same. I could see the hunting dog in her.
The cairn breed springs from hunting terriers capable of
turning a fox or ripping the unfortunate animal to pieces.
I knew Susy had this side to her nature. She didn't know
what fear was.

It was no longer a case of would Susy like her new home
and would the children settle to a life of comparative isolation from neighbours for we all soon became accustomed
to the change. We sometimes strained our ears at night,
listening to the silence, or the intervals of silence between
the hissing of an owl. Often we awoke to a gale that made
the pines lash one another and scatter cones on the roof
and wondered for a moment if the sea had flooded the
whole town. Susy slept through it all, dog-tired. She
needed her sleep for she was bustling about from the
moment we awoke until the day was over. She watched the
children get ready to go to school and would stand for a
few minutes with a plaintive wagging of her tail before
they departed, but as soon as they were gone she would find
something to do in the periwinkle tangle. Sometimes she
would spend a whole morning in there growling, barking,
rushing forward and then waiting for whatever tiny creature she had discovered to make another move and reveal
its presence to her. I would occasionally come home at
lunchtime to be told that she hadn't left the bushes from
the time she had bade us goodbye, but when she heard the
voices of the children she would emerge to greet them, her
body wagged by her tail it seemed.

'Catch a few Sue!' they would cry to set her plunging
back into the bush, and Susy, twice as excited as she had

been in the morning, would hurl herself into the jungle and bark until she was exhausted. A small stone thrown into the bush would set her going again. She hunted by ear, I think, and the stone dropping into the green depths ahead of her sounded like something big enough to get her puppy teeth into. 'Get it Sue!' the children would shout, and the bushes would shake as though Susy had come up with a small tiger and was engaged in a life and death struggle with it. I often thought that this kind of thing is really the fabric of happiness, a complete unawareness of the passing of time with no thought for anything but the thing one is doing. What complicated creatures men have become when they are nagged by things that reduce their concentration and make them incapable of enjoying themselves! What fortunate creatures animals are to be able to groom themselves, oblivious to humans, even to be able to sleep and blot out thought altogether. A built-in clock would tell Susy, the pup, that it was time for her food or time for the car to come rumbling up the lane. She soon learned to know the sound of the engine and would break off what she was doing to come and wait for me after I had put the car in the garage. She never made a mistake and went to greet someone who arrived in another car, even one of the same make.

14

Lost

SOME dogs are demanding because their owners dote over them to an extent that teaches the animal how to get its own way. This is something the simple savage has been known to do to men of considerable intellect and, alas, the victim is never aware that he is being exploited in his weakness. The thing with Susy was that she didn't seem to care. Our affection for her certainly didn't burden her in any way. She could for the most part take us or leave us. When it suited her she would come bustling in like any other member of the family full of enthusiasm for our company and perhaps in her own way trying to communicate her own joy in living. I know she weighed only a few pounds and wasn't six months old when we lost her but her blond coat was growing. She was looking more lovely every day, especially when she posed up among the trees, looking down at us or even putting her forepaws against the trunk of one of the pines and stretching her back. The children would stand in the court admiring her. She seemed to know she was the focus of their attention.

It was after the school term was well under way that prize-giving and speech day came up. I was glad to have an excuse for not attending. Schools, like hospitals, have a certain traumatic effect upon me. I knew too much misery in school to like such places. I am afraid I have never been able to overcome an antipathy towards anyone who tells me he is a schoolmaster, which is something quite irrational. I was glad not to go. My daughter had to go and my wife felt it her duty to show face and support her. There only remained the problem of who would look after the youngest member of the family and Susy, although Susy would be content to hunt the bushes. The chore of guarding the fort and keeping young Ian company fell upon his elder brother. Andrew had no hesitation in volunteering. He hated school almost as much as I had done. Mother and daughter went off to uphold the family name before the staff and the civic dignitaries. Ian played and Andrew pottered and the sun of an Indian summer shone. Susy barked her way into the undergrowth as usual. A few large butterflies hung around the buddleia bushes and blackbirds gorged themselves on over-ripe berries newly touched with frost. The boys were as absorbed in what they were doing as Susy was exploring the endless jungle but then it struck Andrew that he hadn't heard her barking for what seemed a long time! She had gone indoors perhaps? He rushed in. He and Ian made a hurried search under every bed and behind every article of furniture without result. In the normal course of events Susy would have come rushing out to join them and make a game of searching or hunting the house, but the house was now quiet, and empty of any other living creatures. The clock ticked and chimed the quarter-hour, the half-hour, three-quarters and then the hour. They looked in the long greenhouse and the vinery. They searched the most secluded part of the old orchard and the shady places under the pear trees growing against the wall. They called continually. Susy had been known to become so concerned with rooting out a mouse that she would fail to respond to her name, or even hear it. The boys hurried off up into the kitchen garden. They searched for her in the bracken beyond the sundial and through the nettles of the little wood. The wood gave up its pigeons but nothing else. They went on up the cliff path calling her name. She was nowhere to be seen. She was deaf to their calling!

By this time dread had taken the place of anxiety. The boys came down to the court, shut the cottage door and set out to look down the lane. It was a forlorn hope, it seemed, but somehow Susy might have jumped from the wall above our gate and wandered down to meet her mistress. Her existence was a butterfly one in any case. She loved to roam about. This was true, but she was never far from home. She had limits to her territory. She knew where she belonged and she had never strayed before. My wife was coming back home when she met the boys in the lane. Their grave expressions told her there was something wrong. She called to them and they told her that Susy was lost. Susy lost? This couldn't be! Susy was never lost! Susy was always somewhere. Had they left her shut in somewhere? Had they looked down at the bottom end of the potting shed where, in the dark recesses of the cellar-like place below the apple store, there were fieldmice to be cornered? They had looked everywhere, they said. Nevertheless the places they had searched were searched all over again. Four members of the family would search much better than two. Susy would emerge from some bush or remote corner of the jungle, they would see! Everyone began calling Susy's name over again. Tea was forgotten, the house left unguarded. Susy had to be found.

I have always been fascinated by the lost and found column in the local newspaper. I would read a touching request for information about a lost dog or cat, a straying pet or an escaped bird and wonder how people lost things to which they were so patently attached. I still do. I ponder the subject when some farmer enquires about a lost ewe or a pony missing from the grazings. I sigh for the old lady who hopes to find her talking budgie. I know what it is to have lost a pet, a member of the family. I knew it this day when I returned home to find the household in a state of alarm and confusion. No one had eaten. My own appetite disappeared when I heard the news. They were all wrong, of course. Susy couldn't be missing. She was simply occupied digging. Perhaps she was fast in a rabbit hole? I talked about terriers getting stuck in rabbit holes and thought of all the rabbit holes in the wood and along the cliff. I had a slight fear that what I suggested might be true, and we would have a problem on our hands even if we did hear Susy's well-known growling and yelping. I have always had search mania. I am almost incapable of being persuaded to give up looking for something I have mislaid or lost. My father and grandfather suffered from the same ailment. They would turn the house upside down and look in the most ridiculous places for things that eluded them. The family always dreaded telling either of them that something must be listed as lost. It was like saying that something must be considered irrevocably damned to hell. Such pronouncements couldn't be accepted until investigation and the significance of clues put everything to the contrary beyond reason. Susy was not lost, I said, and therefore we had only to find her! No one laughed. I only laughed long afterwards when I recalled how adamant I had been.

We began the search once again, leaving doors and gates open, probing the bushes, flattening the nettles, getting down on our knees and looking into holes, rabbit holes and holes in the limestone walls. I flayed the undergrowth with my stick. I called until I was hoarse. It took me two hours or more to admit that Susy wasn't under the ground or on the ground within our boundary. She must, therefore be outside it. The logic of the remark had long since been considered by the boys. The females of the family had become convinced of the fact long before I accepted it. Now we would spread out and make enquiries throughout the neighbourhood. I would get in touch with the police, but the first thing to do was to get along the lanes, the footpaths and the road, and come up with poor Susy who had wandered and lost her way. After all, she had only been outside our ground in a car. She wouldn't know where she was. She wasn't a homing pigeon or a cat with buttered feet but a small, innocent cairn terrier. The picture was a sentimental one to fit the occasion. Susy was small and perhaps innocent, but she wasn't a fool. She would retrace her steps. She was territorial and the strangeness of a new scene would persuade her to go back the way she had come. The children were almost in tears by this time. The search would go on until we found Susy. Everyone was a little anxious at the thought of night descending before we found our much loved dog.

No one we spoke to remembered seeing a small cairn terrier. A black-faced little dog, was it? they asked, remembering Rory perhaps, and the family's inherited talent for losing dogs. No, we said, a little blond dog, a smiling dog with an undershot jaw, so friendly that she would make a fuss of anyone; a dog among dogs! I thought about an advertisement in the local newspaper—lost on Oct. . . . one small cairn terrier with blond coat, no collar, answering to the name of Susy. . . . reward. But there would be days and nights before the advertisement appeared and perhaps days after that before anyone bothered to read the lost and found column and consider whether or not they had seen a dog with a smile on her face. Susy could have been run over. She had no road sense. She didn't know what a road was! I contacted the local policeman. He rubbed his chin. He would ask around. He couldn't resist the temptation to mention that dogs should have collars and be kept on the lead. If they had a report of a dog being found, handed in, or killed by a car, he would get in touch with me. I felt the way I had felt when the vet was callous about poor Jock's chances of getting over distemper. He would get in touch if someone reported killing a dog on the road! Could he have any conception of what his words meant to us? It was a waste of time talking to him! We needed every minute of daylight remaining but night closed in without news of Susy and we had to give

up. The house was gloomy. We were all depressed beyond
words. It couldn't be true that she had been there at the
beginning of the afternoon, barking joyfully in the bushes,
and now she had vanished from our world without trace.
None of us slept very well. In the night I persuaded myself that I could hear whimpering somewhere outside but
after a long time listening to the hushing of the wind in the
trees I knew I had been mistaken.

The following morning saw us all up and out of bed
earlier than usual. Our fondest hope that Susy would be
sitting on the doorstep wagging her tail wasn't realized.
She wasn't there, nor did she come toddling down from
the bushes, her coat wet with dew. She wasn't out in the
lane. The children went to school dejectedly. My wife re-
sumed the search. I made a tour of the immediate locality
in the car, hurrying if I happened to see a dog turning a
corner, or the tail end of one as it trotted up an alleyway or
along a footpath. We knew where Susy wasn't. What we
needed to know was where she was! The police station
didn't have a dog pound but perhaps someone had brought
Susy in on the end of a piece of string. I called there. The
man on duty took note of what I told him, repeated what
his colleague on the beat had said about collars, leads and
dogs straying on the road. They had no dogs in their back
yard. They had no reports of dogs newly found. People lost
dogs deliberately and dogs were a great nuisance. I didn't
stay to argue the point. I suppose the poor fellow had
enough paperwork to do without making a record of Susy
going walk-about but I couldn't really accept that she had.
It seemed to me that she was too happy at home to wander
as Rory had wandered, but who could steal her from the
ground surrounding the cottage, all of it enclosed by a
man-high limestone wall?

We searched again at the end of the day. We had fewer
people to question for most people we had asked on the
previous day shook their heads and said they hadn't seen
the little dog. It was a shame. Probably picked up and

whisked away by dog-thieves, they said. Dog-thieves and cat-thieves, however, generally have good reason for stealing particular animals, prize-winning, pedigree dogs, or cats they can sell in the fur market. Susy was no glamour dog. A dog-thief wouldn't have looked twice at her to judge what she was worth on the market. She would never be even a runner-up at Crufts as I have said. She was a runt, but the most lovable runt ever whelped, a dog-lover's dog! I didn't think too much about this, but at the end of the day I had lost heart. I told my wife we must consider Susy lost and gone for good. We would never see her again. I was convinced of that. It was no use raising false hopes. It would do no good to advertise in the paper. We should have taken more care of her while we had her. The family went to bed in an even deeper state of gloom than on the night before.

15

. . . And Found

CONSCIENCE is something none of us really needs to cultivate if we look inward. We know what we should do or should have done. Our decisions are often made for us because we don't need to rake over our principles to know what they are. People who lose their dogs often reproach and torment themselves to know the fate of an animal that was important to them. There are people, of course, who stifle their conscience to a horrifying degree and pick up an unwanted dog and throw it away. I always think the latter are people who spend most of their lives escaping from themselves, obliterating the truth, drinking to forget, or throwing themselves into some exhausting business that will guarantee they have no time left for self-examination. We had another day to search both the recesses of the physical world and the depths of our conscience, but really we had done everything to see that a small dog had a happy life and no one could be blamed for her disappearance. Already we were saying we would never have another. The loss was an almost unbearable one. How could Susy have vanished from the face of the earth? The only thing that could account for her disappearance was theft. She must have been stolen. Someone had picked her up and walked away with her, perhaps half-covering her with their coat or popping her in a bag. It would have to be an impulsive theft. I had no sentimental feelings about some poor lonely soul needing a dog for a companion. If the person who had stolen Susy needed something to love they hadn't stopped to think that she was already loved—by an entire family, and all five of us were in misery!

A day of even deeper dejection followed. We were defeated. Everything we had done to find Susy had proved futile. There was no message from the police. No one reported having killed or injured a small dog on the main road or on any of the by-ways. Susy's bed reminded us of the days we had enjoyed her playing and worrying our feet or our slippers. We sighed when we looked at her blanket and the tattered toy dog that she had taken over from the children as her favourite plaything. The telephone didn't ring. We no longer looked for her with any semblance of order or pattern in what we did. The passing of time made it all seem more and more pointless. We were already asking each other if we remembered how Susy liked to do this or that, and recalling the fad she had about drinking water from a bowl—she had to hear the tap running before she would lap from the bowl. The bowl had to be refilled each time before she would drink. This kind of torment was self-indulgence, but we couldn't help ourselves.

My son kept homing pigeons at this time and went to shut them up in the evening and release them in the morning for exercise. He hung about a good deal performing this task, hoping, I am sure, that Susy would suddenly come galloping out of the bushes before he came down for supper, but no such thing happened. One morning Andrew arose as usual and went up to his birds. We were still in bed but felt sure we could hear a sort of whimpering yelp from somewhere up the slope. Could it be Susy? We had imagined such a thing so often in the days since she had gone missing that it was only half-heartedly that I got out of bed and looked up through the pines to the cliff face. Andrew was back from the pigeon loft and frantically scrambling to climb up the ivy on the cliff. It could only mean one thing! Somehow, Susy had come back. It was unbelievable! We rushed downstairs, everyone in a state of great excitement. Susy was crag bound, like a lost sheep, up there on the very precipice. She had come to a dead end and could go neither backwards nor forwards. Andrew was risking his neck to get at her and it wasn't long before he reached her, took her into the crook of his arm and came slipping and slithering down with her. We were choked with emotion. Where had she been? How could she suddently appear up there on the cliff in the early morning? She wasn't wet or bedraggled. She whimpered and cried with delight, but what was it all about?

We never found out, of course. Susy came home, like Lassie, the cynics would say. She had the scent of face powder and the smell of cigarette smoke about her. Whoever had taken her had kept her indoors until that morning. She had probably been kept in a lady's bedroom, cuddled and pampered, I am quite sure. Every dog must be let out once in a while, however, and the moment Susy managed to make her escape she had headed for home—on a beeline! How else could she have come back over the cliff, for on the clifftop, within our stone wall, there is nothing but thorny jungle and tangles of almost impenetrable blackberry and dogrose. To come home she must have followed her nose and burrowed into the bushes and the undergrowth until she emerged on the cliff and found a ledge leading downwards towards the cottage. Here, at last, she had come to the point of no return and had begun to whimper for home was in sight. She must have heard Andrew going up to the pigeon loft and cried when she saw him coming down again.

Susy was brought in like a long lost explorer being welcomed back to camp. She rolled over and rubbed her whiskers on the carpet, barked her delight and forgot her manners. She didn't seem to be hungry but that may have been because she had been overfed or because she was overexcited at being reunited with us again. She was carried upstairs and allowed to sleep on the bed, which she did, sleeping as though she had been travelling all night. Every half hour or so my wife would hurry upstairs to convince herself that it had all happened, and Susy, whom we had thought dead, killed by a car and gone forever, was actually there, curled up on the eiderdown and peacefully sleeping. I telephoned more than once because I too, had a feeling that the whole thing was a dream. I couldn't get over the fact that such a young dog had been able to find her way back across fields and through overgrown places she had never been in before but the homing instinct is not just recognition of landmarks. It depends on the direction of the sun, the angle of light, and perhaps in the case of a dog, the dog's acute sense of smell. If Susy didn't actually scent us she may have recognized the scent of the pine trees, the gorse bushes and perhaps even the smoke from our chimney. Butter the feet of a cat, they say, and the cat will come home. This isn't necessary but the animal's sense of smell guides it from place to place in the blackness of night, even when visibility is down to nothing because of mist or driving rain. I was to find all kinds of things about Susy's sensitivity to things she could not see. I am sure her return home had a great deal to do with a particular super-sensitivity that is in-built in dogs. There would have been nothing so fascinating about her return had she come up the lane and sat on the step by the gate until we found her and brought her in. We wouldn't have known how she had come home at all if she had come down the cliff to the back door. Only because she had been brought to a halt, twenty or thirty feet up the cliff face, had we discovered the way she had come, but nothing could have been more dramatic than her return that morning.

The children fussed over Susy when they returned from school. Susy responded, proving how much she had missed their company. She took a good meal in the late afternoon and basked in our admiration. What had happened was plain. She had gone along the hedge-bottom which flanks the lane. The hedge grows at the top of the limestone wall that marks the boundary of the property. Susy appearing in the tangle of branches head-high above the footpath, must have attracted the attention of someone walking up over the stile. She was the most friendly of pups and would have wagged her tail and made a great fuss of the person who lifted her down. Perhaps they put her on the ground. When she followed them they presumed she was lost, or perhaps they desperately tried to convince themselves that she was lost and must be taken away! However it was, Susy found herself transported far from her own territory and kept a prisoner for several days. Like her journey south, the experience left a mark on her. For days she wouldn't be parted from my wife but kept so close to her she might have been on a string. We had no need to call 'Where's Sue?' Susy was there among us and under our feet, making sure that she didn't lose sight of us, and we didn't lose sight of her.

In the weeks that followed we came to know such a thing wouldn't happen again, and it never did. Susy's character was being formed. She was discriminating between one sort of person and another, one group or unit and her own. It was as though she had become aware of the litter all over again. She began to do her utmost to keep us all together. She was never at rest when one of us was missing and out of her sight. If four of us were in the lounge and one was occupied in the kitchen, doing homework or preparing a meal, Susy would station herself in the hall. Every so often she would bark at the one remaining apart from the rest of the family. She would run to and fro in an effort to keep her eye on all of us and she really tried to shepherd us all into one place. When she achieved this she would rest content, putting her small head on her paws and sleeping but if anyone rose to go off and make tea or something of the kind she would immediately hurry to get the family all in one place again. She had learned something when she went missing. People and dogs get lost and they must contrive to stay together, if they move they should do everything as a pack. I wasn't really aware of this pack instinct in terriers at the time, but some years afterwards I discovered what a force this is. A terrier is not just a hunting dog, for nearly all dogs derive from hunting animals. It is a member of a group. Within the pack there is co-ordinated effort, a single reaction, almost one mind. Five or six Jack Russell terriers become more formidable than an Alsatian. A single terrier, any one taken out of the pack, can be petted and will be a devoted companion but the pack hunts as one and a sort of hunting frenzy transforms every individual into a savage. Susy wasn't in a pack of terriers. She was in a family group and here affection took the place of the hunting and killing which motivates a pack. She nevertheless did her best to 'mother' us, as a bitch controls a litter, and we were always amused and delighted to allow her to do so.

Some time after Susy had returned I saw the local policeman. 'Ever get your dog back?' he asked. I smiled and said I was glad to be able to tell him that we had. He couldn't believe my story of Susy's return but he could speculate as to where she might have been held prisoner. Very, very lucky we were, he said. People don't often recover their dogs and most people don't really care. A dog is easily enticed, especially if it is hungry, or if it happens to be ill-treated at home. I knew Susy didn't come into either of these categories. Friendliness, a gentle nature, had been her undoing. She was above all a most lovable animal. 'Then you make sure you keep a collar on her,' the policeman said, but I wasn't happy about collars on dogs that hunt in bushes. A small dog may easily be caught up by the collar and held fast in undergrowth. At this time we were in the habit of locating Susy almost every half hour of the day. Susy, who had begun to enjoy herself in the bushes as before, would come out of them at the sound of her name. I am sure she knew what it was all about. Both the family and Susy needed reassuring as to the where-abouts of the others. As soon as she had shown face she would turn and go back into the undergrowth and we would get on with whatever we were doing. I often wondered about the people who passed the cottage on their way up the lane to the stile. Among them there may well have been the person who kidnapped Susy. Perhaps Susy knew and barked more fiercely at them than at others who encroached on her territory. Did they say to themselves, 'Look, there's the little dog we stole. I'm glad she went back. She has turned out to be a right little yapper!' I am afraid I never recognized the thief, which was just as well but none of us ever forgot those awful days when we wandered about looking for a dog that had been spirited off the face of the earth.

Susy's life with us was more and more enrichening. We were to remember what happened in puppyhood and adolescence, as we remember the childhood and youth of our children.

16

Top Dog

So imperceptible was Susy's taking over the family that I am hard put to it to say exactly when it began. Perhaps it began immediately she was restored to us. I fancy we placed her on a pedestal from that day onwards. Perhaps we gave in and became her willing slaves immediately. Outsiders may have it their way and say it was the day we lost our reason, collectively, like the Gaderine swine. No one ever regretted it happening. We didn't really care whether outsiders smiled or sneered at our concern for a small dog. She was terribly important to us and everything she did fascinated us more than the behaviour of most of our visitors and many of our friends. We looked inwards and were enchanted. Susy loved being with us and we loved being with her. If anyone was the least inconsiderate towards her the others would reproach him. Susy was never left out or forgotten. Even when we had some special treat Susy had to be offered a share. I think it was at this time that she sat up and begged without anyone having taught her the trick. Most intelligent dogs do this without being taught to sit up but I think begging is only the tip of the iceberg, indicating that the dog knows human weakness and how to make the most of it. We would be sitting at dinner on Sunday and someone would exclaim 'Oh look at Sue!' and Susy would improve upon her begging posture by pawing the air with both feet together. No one could tell me she didn't know what she was doing! The gesture was quite irresistible. No one could refuse her the titbit she wanted and she always took the offering very gently and delicately, refusing if it we offered her anything large that might have to be gulped down or broken up on the carpet. 'Isn't she lovely!' we would exclaim. She didn't repeat her supplicating gesture. In fact, unless we had something she couldn't resist she would toddle off and lie down. It was as though she exacted a token from us and once it had been given she was satisfied that we hadn't forgotten her and still worshipped her.

All dogs are creatures of habit. What they become accustomed to doing they will expect every day of their lives. They will watch for some indication that soon a meal will be produced, or shortly we will go for a walk. Susy's walks were ritual. She loved to go the same way and she would stop at the same places to sniff her landmarks. There was a great rock up on the clifftop with a depression in it that always collected rainwater. She would wind her way up the cliff path, following the ancient sheep tracks that flocks had used since time immemorial, reach the fine grass on the clifftop, and trot to the rock so that she could drink from that cup of pure rainwater. Only in very dry seasons was she disappointed and she would stop and turn her head as though seeking some explanation as to why the depression in the rock had no water in it. She would go for her walk, hail, rain or shine and loved nothing better than snow on the ground. She may have been tenderfooted because most of our ground is stony and rough. When it snowed she could hardly wait to get outside and she would be gone for ages, collecting balls of snow on the long fur of her underbelly and around her hindquarters, some of them much bigger than golf balls. We would spend a long time melting the snow off her hair and drying her thoroughly, but at the earliest opportunity she would be off out again, galloping through the snow and snuffling into it when she got the scent of a rabbit, a mouse or perhaps a starving redwing wretchedly waiting for death at the coming of night.

Knowing how much she loved the snow we took her on one occasion for a walk in the mountains. The crags and rock faces were sheathed in ice. We walked part of the way almost knee-deep in snow across which Susy raced like a miniature husky, keeping ahead of us and continually looking back and barking to make sure we kept going. She always hated to lag behind and could hardly bear to be anything but the leader of the pack. On this day we all overdid it, for the snow was deep and the route we had chosen was a hairpin one, as fatiguing to turn back upon as to go on. Susy made the pace for more than two hours. I couldn't possibly work out how many paces her short legs took to our one, for she never slowed down enough for me to work it out, but at last even Susy had to give up and she stopped on a snowy bank to wait for us. I could see her when I was about two hundred yards from her. She was exhausted and she was telling me so by sitting on her hind legs, begging to be lifted and carried the rest of the way! She was a most touching sight and as always, utterly irresistible. One of the boys floundered forward and swept her up into his arms. She was content to go back to the car as a drop-out. She had galloped over the snow for something close to five miles and we were concerned for her as well as proud of her. Ask any member of the family now grown to manhood about the things Susy did and they will tell you about her great trek across the frozen wastes and how she lay sleeping afterwards.

Playing is as essential to a dog as it is to a human. All dogs love to play and enjoy mock battles, competition of one sort or another in obtaining possession of a ball, a stick or some other plaything. Susy played, even when she was an octogenarian. As a young dog she had special playthings. She would spend hours tossing or throwing about my son's collection of clear glass marbles but someone always had to compete with her for the marbles. She lost interest if no one seemed to want to deprive her of them. She loved to play the same game with a grape and would gently pick it up and toss it across the carpet and look from it to whoever was at hand. It only needed the slightest movement on the part of the onlooker to have Susy bounding towards the grape which she would throw over her shoulder or flick off under some article of furniture. Only when the grape was broken would she give up. Most of the time the grape became a prize titbit and she would eat it, but she never seemed to want a grape if anyone refused to take part in a game. She would leave it lying on the floor as though to say if we didn't want to play the thing could remain where it was until someone put their foot on it and trod it into the carpet. Only strangers missed the point. We knew how to play up to her just as she knew how to play up to us. Again, we couldn't pretend we were normal when we had company and Susy came forward with either a marble or a grape in her mouth. 'You'll excuse me,' I would say, 'but this is one of Susy's favourite games.' Our visitors had to take us as they found us.

I remember one occasion when Susy was worked up about a blue-bottle that had come in through the open window. She sat looking at the large fly high up on the wall and a guest who wasn't particularly observant asked what was wrong with the little dog, sitting bristling and so intent upon something. 'She has her eye on that fly,' I said. The guest nodded but looked rather baffled. The fly took off. Susy barked and dashed round the room like a mad thing, snapping her jaws and growling. Our visitor raised an eyebrow. 'She's a great fly-hunter,' I said rather feebly. I couldn't say she was a great fly-catcher for she hardly ever caught these tantalizing flies. Our calmness in the face of such upheaval and excitement must have made most of our visitors wonder about us! Susy would knock over a small table, bring a lamp crashing to the floor and almost trip my wife bringing in a tray of tea. We thought nothing of it. It was her way! If she was eccentric we loved her eccentricity and we insisted she was a dog of character, which she was, by any standard.

Nick, nack pallywag, give a dog a bone had been one of the chants of my childhood and I would often bring home a large bone for Susy, a bone as big as herself on some occasions. Susy wasn't really a great worrier of bones. I think her undershot jaw had something to do with this shortcoming. She would gnaw the prized bone for a short time and then carry it about looking for somewhere to bury it. When we noticed that she was intent upon interring the bone we would quickly open the door and let her out. She was very selective in her burying places and would trot about for ages, trying to make up her mind the best place to use as a larder, but once the place was decided upon she would bury the bone and come indoors, dirty-faced and whiskered with pine needles. Dozens of times she would sneak back out and recover the bone without our being aware of the fact and the next thing we knew the chosen member of the family would come down after bidding us goodnight carrying a very earthy bone between finger and thumb. This was the supreme mark of favour so far as Susy was concerned. She gave her bone to the particular member of the family upon whom she was lavishing her affection at that time, putting the offering under the counterpane of their bed or burying it deep between the sheets. The bone would be taken outside and disposed of, but if Susy happened to notice it being thrown away she gave no sign. It was enough, I suppose, that the chosen one appreciated he or she was favoured. Susy had nothing else to give.

When by accident Susy found herself shut out of the lounge or the dining-room, both of which happen to have plate glass panelled doors, she would stand and stare in at us, seeming to look reproachful until someone noticed her and went to let her in, but if no one noticed she would strike at the plate glass with her paw. Everyone in the room would look round, full of reproach for whoever had shut poor Susy out. She was very good at throwing a partially closed door back by striking it with her paw, but we always begged her to learn to close doors as efficiently as she opened them. She ignored us and never made the slightest attempt to shut the door behind her. Now, when she has been dead almost a year we look at the marks of her claws on all the wooden doors. They remind us of her impatience to be inside with us, or off to her bed which was her sanctum sanctorum to which she would resort wherever it happened to be, out in the courtyard, in the middle of the lounge, or on the back seat of the car. She was like a small child and had what we called her cuddly, a steadily diminishing fragment of cellular blanket with which she would make her bed over and over again. All dogs go through a ritual of lying down to sleep, turning round and round and making themselves confortable. It is said that this dates from the days of the cave or before. Susy would do this but she would also make her bed, tugging and pulling at her blanket, getting right out of bed and sorting it all out rather ineffectually before getting back in again and attempting to get comfortable. No one ever attempted to make her bed for her while she was so busy but after she had settled down she would permit my wife to straighten things up and tuck her in. Soon she would be snoring.

The children loved these 'character' antics. They stood around fascinated to see Susy being herself, and she was herself above all, completely absorbed in doing what she was doing, whether it was bed-making or grooming herself, which she did frequently to an extent that she often choked on the hair she had combed. When the children went off to school she would sleep, but when the youngest had to go to school she must have felt that most of the litter was missing. For days on end she made strenuous efforts to go with them. More than once she jumped down from the court into the lane and tore off after them. The jumping alarmed me for I had known gundogs twist their intestines and die when they landed badly. Susy desperately wanted to go where the children went. She wasn't quite as popular as she might have been when one or other of them discovered that they had been followed and had to pick her up and carry her home again. We were no longer afraid that Susy would go missing but our great anxiety was that in her frantic dash to catch up she would run across the path of a car and be killed. I altered the fence along the top of the wall, bending a section of weldmesh to prevent Susy reaching the place from which she made her leap. After that she couldn't tag along, but she would stand with her forepaws on the weldmesh weeping pitifully to be allowed to go to school. It was a long time before she gave up trying and resignedly took her farewell of the children at the gate before coming indoors to sleep and forget. When they came home she danced round them and would sit up for a share of their chocolate cake, which she loved as much as they did. No matter how hungry they were, or how much they loved cake, Susy was always given her share. A piece of cake to herself wasn't enough. She had to exact tribute from the other members of the litter!

17

The Hunting Dog

WE had had myxomatosis and the horrors of the rabbit plague a short time before we moved to the cottage, but soon, it seemed, the ravages of the disease would be forgotten. The rabbit population flourished again. Rabbits began infiltrating the defences of the kitchen garden. There were young ones everywhere, dashing from bush to bush, bobbing along the top of the cliff and even, at times, venturing so close to our door that I hesitated to shoot them from the bathroom window for fear of mutilating them and making them useless for the pot. Susy loved stewed rabbit. We didn't really fancy it any more. What Susy liked, even more than eating rabbit as fine as breast of chicken, was hunting rabbits. She would get beside herself with excitement when she put one out of a bush. Her small legs would move so quickly that she didn't get off immediately but hung there like a car with wheelspin, over-revving at take-off. Sometimes she waltzed sideways, growling and barking to catch up. Sometimes she crashed into bushes and collided with trees in her frenzy to get her teeth into an escaping rabbit. When she was in one of these hunting fits she was oblivious to everything else and everyone about her. We could call, cajole, command, but she would be completely deaf to our entreaties. In a few seconds she must have burned thousands of calories and taken years off her life, I always felt. If I ever managed to pick her up I would find her shaking with excitement, breathing like a small steam engine at full throttle, her heartbeats almost merging into one another. She wasn't the dog that slept nose-to-tail in the warmth of her bed, the gentle little creature that licked my hand. She licked only very special people; I was one of those she washed as she washed herself. Perhaps she thought there was something lacking in my conception of personal cleanliness!

It needed no encouragement to have Susy tearing away after a real or imaginary rabbit, but what did it every time was the sound of a gunshot. Without being introduced to the gun Susy knew that a gunshot meant that something had been brought down. That something might be a rabbit, a woodpigeon or a pheasant. All of these were likely to come picking or nibbling at the greenstuff I was growing in the kitchen garden. If a pigeon happened to flutter on the ground Susy would race in and seize it. If a rabbit happened to be wounded she was on its trail through the nettles before I could get there, but she never savaged the kill. When she discovered that it was incapable of response she would sniff at it and even lick it. She did the same thing whenever I happened to have a cut on my hand. I am quite sure this was to salve the wound and an instinctive reaction to the smell or taste of blood. I never managed to conceal a cut finger from Susy and she would lick a wound unless forcibly prevented from doing so. My wife would complain if I happened to slip out in the early morning to shoot a rabbit or a pigeon, not so much because she disapproved of my killing things, which she did, even when the vegetable garden was being ruined, but because I left Susy indoors. Susy would be so enthusiastic to get to the scene of operations that she would race ahead and my pests would take flight or scuttle away before I could bring the gun to bear upon them. To avoid this I would put the gun together as quietly as I could and load it with the click of its closing muffled, for if Susy heard the gun being closed she would come racing down to join me. Once outside I would make my stalk and shoot whatever was on the cabbage patch. The gunshot would startle the sleeping family, but even more startling would be Susy's frantic racing about to find a way out, to say nothing of her yelping and barking! Sometimes I would be on my way back to the house before Susy could be released and she would race up to me, jumping on her hind legs to be allowed to lick or smell whatever it was I had killed. This was one of her delights when I had been away shooting on one of the Anglesey farms or marshes where we rented some sporting rights. I always had to lay out my bag and let Susy inhale the exciting scents of pheasant, partridge, woodcock or duck. She would spend a long time over them, like a woman in a perfume shop and I had to let things lie until she had done with them, or she would trail after me out to the potting shed, intoxicated by the smell of a long-legged marsh hare, or a widgeon which has a much more oily smell than a mallard.

'Couldn't you take Susy with you just once?' my wife would ask. I sometimes wish I had done, although, stout-hearted and tough though she was, the expedition could have been too much for her heart. There was hardly a day when I didn't wade almost knee-deep in moss and rushes or walk through tall kale and the mud would have been too much for a small, short-legged dog like Susy. Susy had to be content with hunting on her own, except on rare occasions when she was a real asset in getting a bird out of a bush or flushing a rabbit. She didn't grieve over something she had never known, of course, and she was in her seventh heaven when I did come into the house and call her to help me. Nothing could hold her back. She would slip and slide on the polished floor, fall over and scramble to her feet again to rush after me. She knew what it was about, and there was nothing that gave her more pleasure. I would say that she was a great huntress without catching very much. Occasionally she caught a mouse. She sometimes caught a bluebottle and coughed and choked to eject it from her mouth, but what she loved was the chase rather than the kill. Looking back at it, now that I have given up killing things, I think this is what it was really about as far as I was concerned. I too, preferred the chase to the kill, the stalk to the capture, luring a fish rather than netting it out of the water.

The sound of the gun excited Susy until she was an old dog and her hearing dulled and her legs became stiff, but when she was in her 'teens' the children were sometimes encouraged by every wile Susy possessed when she wanted to hunt rabbits. She would run to and fro, trying to direct their footsteps towards the cliff and the jungle at the top. My son Andrew who loved this game as much as Susy once took her away up to the tower so that she could explore the bushes and the secret paths under the old blackthorns and wind-laid larches. Susy trundled in and out, excited by every new scent she discoverd until all at once she was missing. Where had she gone? Andrew followed the path she had taken and discovered that Susy had gone to earth. She had forced her way into a rabbit hole but what was much more serious, the rabbit hole was a tunnel in the old limestone where she might get stuck. Andrew waited anxiously for Susy to emerge. Susy struggled on. Where would she come out? Old rabbit tunnels on the cliff had largely fallen into disuse after the plague. Rabbits did go below ground, but survivors really lived on the surface, on hedge-banks and in sheltered places deep under bushes. At last Susy came ploughing out of a hole some distance from the one she had entered. Red brown earth covered her back. She was a sorry sight until she shook herself and looked about to get her bearings. She had no idea of the anxious moments she had given Andrew. Dogs live for the moment and fear is not something that enters their heads until they are physically threatened. It had all been a matter of burrowing along in the dark and going forward where she couldn't turn back. At the end of it all she found herself in the fresh air with a canopy of sticks and greenery above her. What was there to be frightened about after all?

Every year when the shooting season begins on the adjoining estate we get a procession of pheasants, coming in ones and twos from a wood over on the other side of the cliff. These are birds that have an ancient escape route which even the keepers don't seem to have located. I have counted as many as twenty cock pheasants crossing the wall in a matter of an hour or two. The birds file back again after the tumult and the shouting has died, but slowly, in their own time, since no one drives them back. When I first came to the cottage I regarded these migrants as a small bonus for owning a freehold adjacent to an estate. I could stock my larder with pheasants if I felt so inclined, although there was little sport in shooting birds I hadn't stalked through a marsh or walked up in a field of kale. I took the bounty nature and the gamekeepers seemed to offer. One winter I shot no less than thirty-six cock pheasants on the kitchen garden, all of them birds that took flight for our boundary, up over the wych elms. A pheasant feeding on an open field isn't easily taken. It has such acute hearing that it will detect the closing of a door, the click of a gun being loaded, and the footsteps of a man walking on grass in his slippers. More often than not the birds I saw gorging themselves on my winter vegetables slipped off into the little wood and were lost before I knew they had gone. One morning, however, when I particularly wanted a cock pheasant, a plump and quite splendid bird went quietly up past the old sundial and seemed in no hurry at all. I looked out and took note of his route. I knew he would soon find cover in the little wood and hurry up the inside of the limestone wall to a place where stunted bushes and old ivy mantle the rock. I called Susy and for once she came without barking and yelping.

'Quietly now, Sue,' I told her. 'Quietly, there's a good dog.'

I suppose my mood was somehow transmitted to the little dog. She looked up at me and wormed herself alongside my feet as I walked past the sundial. She knew what it was about! Softly, softly, catchee monkey! We went on through the gap into the wood. The old red cock scuttled and scampered to get uphill and found cover before he needed to take flight. I told Susy to go up and put him out of that. Like a well-trained gundog she went out and round to cut him off. She scuttled and scampered even more than he had done, and now she gave a little yelp, which was all to the good because the bird would have some idea of the danger on the way to the very top of the wood. He turned and went across the slope lower than Susy. If she didn't see him, she must have either heard or scented him, for she turned and angled down towards him. I thought it would only be a minute before he took wing, but instead, judging he was much faster than a mere terrier, he doubled back. Susy skidded round on a sort of scree of thick pine needles and went after him. I slipped the safety catch off the gun but I had no intention of shooting until the bird was in the air, or shooting at an angle which might cause pellets to rattle off a pine tree and hit the dog. Pheasants often clap down a moment before they take flight. This one did. Susy stopped and looked down at me for a second or two before she scented him. A pheasant can close its wings and prevent its strong game smell betraying it, but it can't wipe a trail out of the air. Susy followed on like any well-trained spaniel. I was very proud of her and quite fascinated to see that she seemed to know what she was doing. I suppose we all tend to think that a small dog, with a small brain, is at some disadvantage when it comes to working things out, but nothing could be farther from the truth. Susy tracked uphill and in a moment came to a halt right where the pheasant crouched in the stunted blackberry. She growled. I could hear her perfectly in the quietness of the wood. Less than half a minute later I was startled by the clatter of the cock's wings as one invariably seems to be. He rose, turned to find a way through the tops of the pines, and I fired. He came down rather like a falling leaf. I knew at once what that meant. I had winged him and he was almost certainly capable of running as fast as a hare. Susy hadn't taken her small, sharp eyes off him for an instant. He dropped and she was there, fastening herself to him while he fluttered and flapped. I struggled uphill and she held on. In no time she had given up the bird and was watching me make a quick end of it, but how proud she was of our joint effort. How she tried to dance round me as I carried the bird, its head through the fingers of my left hand, as I made my way to the bottom of the wood and the footpath there.

I don't think Susy was ever quite so pleased with herself or with me. When she was really delighted at anything she would raise her muzzle like a baying hound and make a sort of half-growling noise in her throat, a croon of pleasure. I praised her all the way down to the cottage. She had performed like a true hunter.

18

Crisis

THE trouble with dogs is that they can't communicate but we often used to say that if Susy could talk we wouldn't get a word in edgeways. She did her best to talk and I am sure that sometimes she thought we were very dull if we couldn't understand what she meant. We had learned what she meant when she growled for a drink of fresh water. She would never be content with water already in the dish. We knew she was dropping hints about suppertime from around five o'clock onwards. Her appetite was wonderful. She wasn't greedy, but she loved her food. Her nose was always moist and her vitality was inexhaustible. From morning until night she was a bustling, busy dog. I won't say that she planned her day. She played it by ear. I think. Certainly she made plenty of noise when she was excited and busy, and would involve anyone in what she was doing, drawing them into a chase after a bee or a butterfly or hunting a mouse. It was impossible not to become involved when she took off round the dining-room in pursuit of a bee or a wasp because there was a great danger of Susy getting stung around the mouth. A wasp can sting more than once and might even kill a dog if it happened to sting it in the throat. Susy forgot about wasps and bees until she caught one and then she made frantic efforts to get the thing out of her mouth. We told her about it, but she never remembered! An exchange of ideas would have helped. I might have been able to tell her the difference between a bluebottle, a bee, and a wasp, but communication was limited to 'Catch one Sue!' if the thing happened to be a bluebottle, or 'No Sue! No!' when it was a wasp. It was this lack of communication that brought us to the trauma of Susy's first serious illness. She had been such an active, lively dog that we couldn't think of her being ill or off colour. She had little fads so far as food was concerned and didn't show much enthusiasm when tinned dog foods of certain famous brands were put down for her, but who would when they could expect lamb's liver one day, stewing beef the next and tender hearts, boiled until they were as appetizing as veal?

We took Susy wherever we went and she was only rarely left alone in the house and never for very long. She didn't like being left behind and would happily sleep in the car if we visited a household where there was a dog already in residence. We took her on picnics, as most people who love dogs will, although we were always careful to picnic in places where a dog wouldn't be a nuisance to those who might not welcome them or where there was livestock. Susy suffered from an uncontrollable curiosity. No cat was ever more curious. She just had to investigate. She wouldn't chase sheep but she would approach them and stand and stare. When we had sheep here she had been put out when a ewe stamped her foot at her and ran towards her with her head down, like a ram about to charge, but this didn't mean she had lost her courage. She loved to study any kind of animal we encountered. We took her to the moor because she loved such places. Perhaps something about the moor harked back to her infant nature in the far-off Highlands. She was transported with joy when she could bundle through tall heather and scramble over peat banks. We supposed the air did as much for her as it did for us. If Susy suffered from nostalgia on the moor, so did I. I have always loved the scent of moss, bog myrtle, heather and

peat. I day-dream when I hear the curlew's cry or see a
raven going slowly across the wild countryside. We took
Susy for a picnic one warm summer's day when she was
eleven years old, making the journey to a moorland plateau
in Snowdonia in the company of friends. We had brought
Susy's dish, her bed, her meal, and a bottle of water from
which we could pour her a drink. Susy seemed a little overcome with the heat that summer afternoon. We decided
that there hadn't been enough fresh air getting into the
car. She would be fine once she was out among the heather.
We parked on a piece of hard ground off the mountain track
and set up our stools and the folding table. The sun blazed
down. There was a shimmering haze over the high peaks.
Sheep bleated and fat old bumble bees droned across the
moorland looking for some sign that the heather buds were
about to break into bloom. A skylark rose. A wheatear
posed on a lichened rock. Susy was looking for shade. She
wasn't at all excited by the butterfly that fluttered over the
car. I remember seeing the way she looked at it and thinking, well, she wasn't as young as she had been. None of us
were. I had debated whether I would join the syndicate
who shot over one of the moors a few miles across country.
It is a very strenuous business walking a moor in August
to put up a few unkeepered grouse. I too, was feeling my
age.

Late in the afternoon Susy declined her food. Well, it
was the heat of the day that had put her off. She would eat
later on. She trundled off and began to dig in the peat. I
was reassured. She had always been a great digging dog.
She would have her food when she had used her energy
digging a hole. Susy dug without great enthusiasm and lay
down where she had excavated a cool place in a narrow
depression in the peat bank. It was natural that she wanted
somewhere more pleasant than the shelter of an oily car or
even the interior of a car which, as the afternoon had pro-
gressed, had become as hot as a baker's oven. We lazed
and talked and took a short stroll. The day was perfect.

Susy would be herself when we got home. We all had off days, didn't we? Susy didn't take her food, even when we got home but she was very thirsty. That was natural, however. A dog doesn't perspire, but it loses body fluid on a very hot day and we had never been too enthusiastic about trimming her coat or having her plucked. Poor little thing, she had to go out in a heavy overcoat in high summer. It was all wrong. We should have had it done, as we had on previous occasions. All this was to cover a nagging doubt that Susy was quite herself. She left her supper untouched. We knew she would be ravenous tomorrow and would dance around on her hind legs, begging for an extra meal. The untouched food was thrown away. In the morning she wouldn't be tempted with the best titbits we could find. She would only drink. Well, we said for the hundredth time, a dog knows when it is hungry and when it doesn't want food. A few hours without food would do no harm at all.

A day passed and Susy wouldn't even sniff at the choicest things we put before her. She loved meat. She wolfed chicken, but now she would have none of it. We hovered over her. She wagged her tail and trotted about, but without her usual exuberance. Had I watched her as closely as she had watched me from the time she had joined the family I would have been able to tell that she was seriously ill. If she seemed to be reasonably active and not completely lethargic this was just her indomitable spirit. She was a brave little animal, not given to moping or appearing sorry for herself. Another day without food and yet another and we decided that she would have to go to the vet. I don't think we had had her to the vet in all her eleven years. I fancy she had had all her injections at the outset, although I may be wrong about this. We put her on the seat of the car and went off to take our place in the vet's long queue.

The pet world is full of people who have soft hearts, people who love dogs and become so deeply involved with them that they are incapable of seeing that their behaviour is anything but normal. Apart from the dog farmers, the breeding fraternity who can be quite callous about an animal, the 'doggie' world is one of sympathy and understanding and quite unashamed sentimentality! We were surprised to see that we were not the only ones who were deeply concerned because a hitherto lively dog had gone off its food. We sympathized with people we had never met before, people who were grief stricken at the thought that their old dog had come to the end of the line, and people who had a look of doom on their faces because their pet had a tumour. Susy was just off her food, we said as we waited. Susy took it all very calmly. The vet summoned us into his surgery and put Susy on the table, asking one of us to hold her by the head while he examined her. I felt this was nonsense. Susy would hardly harm a fly, I said. The vet shook his head. He wasn't denying that Susy was a gentle creature. His expression was grave. She was seriously infected internally, he said. She was inclined to drink a lot, wasn't she? We couldn't deny that she was. It was a certain sign, he told us. It would be as well to limit her drinking. He would give her a large injection of antibiotic and see her again the following day. A series of three large injections might do what was needed. If this failed an operation would be needed. How old was she? We told him. He looked grave again. It would be like operating on an old lady of eighty, he said. For the first time I really knew that Susy wasn't a young dog. She had bundled and bounced her way through life, growing old with us. The thought that she might not survive an operation, or that she needed one, hadn't entered my head. The vet's verdict came like a bombshell. We went home considerably shaken, willing Susy to recover after the first big injection, which, I am sorry to say, made her cry out like a small child.

We couldn't make her take her food on the following day. She seemed to be trying to please us by sniffing at the contents of her dish. We took her back for her second injection, smiled weakly at the same faces and waited our turn. There was no lack of sympathy. The vet was a most wonderful man, they said, a man with the greatest sympathy for living things. He could work miracles. The second injection appeared to have no more effect upon Susy's condition than the first. The third didn't make her eat, nor did it diminish her thirst. The vet told us that he would have no alternative but to operate. There was nothing else that could be done but to leave the dog to die. What were the chances? He looked gravely at us. He wasn't prepared to speculate until he had opened her up. It all depended upon how seriously she was infected, and whether her heart was strong enough to stand the shock of an operation. She seemed a dog with a good consitution. If she was 'clean' internally there was every reason to hope that she could come through. We brought her to his surgery at the beginning of the afternoon and left her to be dealt with in due course. We were very pessimistic and went away sunk in gloom. We talked about all the things Susy had done, all the occasions when she had made us laugh, and the mischief she had got into. We remembered our agony when she was missing and the way she would rush after me when she heard me fire a shot. It was the longest day in our lives, the day when Susy went under the knife. We couldn't bring ourselves to stand by the telephone nor could we bear to sit at home. We went off for a short run in the car and reluctantly had a meal of tea and scones, the first thing I had eaten for three days. How could a small dog have taken such a hold upon me, I wonder? I can only admit that she had. I had lost my reason somewhere along the way, but then the same thing had happened to every member of the family. We telephoned the news of crisis to everyone concerned before Susy was left at the surgery. Now we would be expected to telephone the outcome and I hardly had the courage to ring the vet. When I did I was told that an emergency had prevented him from operating until much later than he had planned.

There was nothing to be said for the time being. I found it even harder to enquire on the second occasion, but when I did I was relieved to hear that it was all over. The operation was successful this far. Susy had come round. We could come and get her. I was amazed as well as relieved, for I had fancied that Susy would remain at the surgery for several days, but we wasted no time and hastened to the car and drove to the vet's place. What would she look like? I imagined she would lie limp and lifeless and we would lift her gently into her bed and transport her home.

The vet was quite cheerful. She was clean inside, he said, meaning that he had found no malignant growths. He had performed a hysterectomy and had removed no less than 'a bucketful of pus' from Susy's infected organs. She couldn't have lived more than a few hours. Now she would recover—with care and attention. He opened a door and Susy wobbled out to meet us, her eyes not really focussing properly, her tail wagging just a little because she recognised the sound of our voices.

19

The Patient's Relapse

WE were quite overwhelmed to have her with us once more, so much that we didn't see what we didn't want to see. She had come through the operation well enough. Her constitution was good, but she had been seriously infected, and it was the extent of that infection that the vet was concerned about when he told us to keep a careful eye on her. We knew about her wanting to drink. That was a sign of continued infection. Her whole system had begun to be affected and no animal can live with its bloodstream heavily infected. But this was Susy, the idol of the family. She was indestructible! She wouldn't die and leave us. The vet didn't know what strength and courage she had. The vet, however, wasn't giving his verdict on the first dog he had ever operated upon, or the first he had ever stood on his table for examination. It was no use our singing the old jazz song about knowing Susy like we knew Susy. We were made to think again before twenty-four hours had passed. She wouldn't eat. She wanted water. She didn't brighten up, even at home where she belonged, but wanted to sleep. It was going to be too much for her! Hadn't the vet said something about an operation on a very old lady? He had, however, told us that he expected to give her another five years of life if she came through the operation! We took Susy back the following day. Once again the vet got out his needle and gave her a large dose of antibiotic. She had eaten nothing since long before her operation. We were all anxious about her strength. We bought almost everything a sick dog might be tempted with, but Susy didn't brighten up or show the slightest interest in food. We didn't know then that dogs can last much longer than humans without going under. She was drinking of course, although she seemed to want to do nothing but rest. We took her to the vet again and he boosted the antibiotic charge. I was beginning to get despondent. He could give her only one more injection and the crisis of a couple of days before would be upon us once more, this time without hope of anything to be done.

The antibiotic at last began to work for Susy drank less. I devoted my mind to ways in which I could stimulate her appetite. She loved to lick my hand. I let her lick my fingers and dipped them in a thick gruel which she licked away. Almost at once she began to perk up and improve! Now we watched over her with the attention of parents with a sick child. Susy, who still suffered from what the knife had done and the stitching its use had entailed, did her best to respond. She even managed a slight bark, but she didn't bark loudly or strongly. I suppose the effort of barking hurt her healing wound or made the stitches drag. She didn't need to be taken to the vet now. She was on the mend. The first real sign of recovery she gave was to sit up to be lifted up on to the bed. I don't think she had ever done anything that touched me more. I looked at her wobbling uneasily with her paws drooping and I shouted to the family to let them know she was herself again before bending down and lifting her where she wanted to be. We watched to see if she would want to drink more than usual. We measured and studied her every meal. We hardly let her out of our sight but trotted after her to see what she was up to, even when all she wanted was to snooze under a table or find a cool place in which to lie down for a while. Isn't she wonderful, we asked one another, able to come through a major operation at the age of eighty! We ignored the fact that she was 11, going 12. She wasn't a mere dog. She was one of us, as much loved as a grandmother or grandfather!

I suppose Susy rediscovered how important she really was to us, and what was her right. She basked in the sunshine of our smiles but she took it all with regal dignity. One or the other of us would step aside for her, open a door for her when she wanted to go somewhere. I would swear that sometimes she headed for the door just to see what power she had over us. 'Susy wants to come in,' someone would say, rushing to open the door, and Susy would hesitate and turn and go the other way. 'Susy wants to go out!' but Susy would simply sniff the air outside and turn around and amble back to her cushion. Someone would come downstairs and sit on the settee and those in armchairs would look up and remark, 'That's Susy's chair!' The mad thing was that no one objected. No one said that humans came before a mere dog, for this was no mere dog. This was a very special animal, not just a pampered terrier. Susy didn't sulk, didn't whine and didn't take advantage in the way pampered animals tend to do, but accepted us as we accepted her. To her we were still members of the litter. Was it so extraordinary that we regarded her as one of us?

When the day came for the last of her stitches to be removed we were anxious for her. My wife had gone to London on a visit. Ian and I took Susy to the vet, a feeling growing within us as we drove the five or six miles that Susy would be frightened and distressed to enter the surgery. Susy was quiet enough on the journey, but she knew where she was when we trundled up the rough road to the surgery and came to a halt. There were other cars already parked. People with ailing dogs waited for the vet to finish his lunch and take his daily surgery. Susy was uneasy. I talked to her, but it did nothing to calm her. She could smell the antiseptic. She could remember the needles and the unavoidable pain she had suffered. At last our turn came. I picked her up, walked in and put her on the table. The vet smiled cheerfully at us. 'Good for another five years with any luck!' he said. 'She has made a fine recovery. She is a healthy little thing.' I helped hold her while he cut away the insoluble stitches. Susy cried like a child that had hurt itself, once, twice, three times. It was awful to listen to but it was soon over. She was shivering and trembling when I took her out and back to the car, but in a little while the ordeal was forgotten. We drove home thinking of the years the vet had promised her, thankful that we had found a man who really cared about animals and knew exactly how to treat them. We received the bill a few days later. It was so modest we felt he must have made a mistake. We would have paid him anything he had asked, of course.

The relapse had been much more wearing on our nerves than the ordeal of the operation which had preceded it, but now that Susy was on her feet we could breathe again. Susy's recovery was quite wonderful. Animals heal quickly and aren't plagued with anxiety about things that are behind them. Susy would come in from the garden, bustling and growling her delight and immediately set her nose under the edge of a large carpet which covered the fitted carpet in the dining-room, and roll it back a couple of yards if she could, or burrow away underneath it making a tunnel to the other side of the room and sometimes knocking furniture over in the process. She could run upstairs again and did so at the same mad gallop. She would sit on her favourite step and put her head through the rails of the stair so that she could look down through the dining-room window at the lane. This was part of her watchdog duty, it seemed. She would wait for hours on end for someone to come along the footpath and bark for an hour after they had gone. Nothing could make her stop. If the passer-by loitered Susy would rush down the steps, turn the corner at the bottom at high speed and go racing through to the kitchen to be let out. If she was ignored she would bark even louder and growl her indignation. We simply had to let her out. I was always a little self-conscious about this for it must have seemed that we were 'letting the dog loose' to the person looking up at the pine trees or admiring the daffodils above the court. Sometimes I would rather shame-facedly go out and explain that she was a mad little dog but wouldn't hurt a fly. She just got over-excited at times! Dog-lovers understood, I suppose, but some of the passers-by must have thought poor Susy a clamorous, ill-tempered little bitch, which was far from the truth. Let out into the lane she would rush to the stranger wagging her tail, a complete contradiction of herself a moment or two before!

Susy had been belatedly 'neutered' but it had no noticeable effect on her psychological make-up. Long before she had come to this physcial crisis she had been strangely aggressive with most male dogs and more than aggressive with females. Our neighbour's bitch had one day wandered through and encountered Susy on the path. Susy met her match and was badly bitten under one eye. We heard her whimpering in time to rush and prevent more serious injury, but this brush with a member of her own sex did nothing to deter her when she met a dog in the lane. There was only one dog that pleased her, a bright, lean little Aberdeen terrier with whom she would frolic and gambol like a pup. Alas, Susy's sweetheart died young and she never took another. She would see off Doctor Boney's big, friendly boxer named Brutus. Brutus would come rushing up into the court if the gate had been left open and Susy would take off like an electric hare, skidding to get at him while he, with his stump tucked in, would go crashing down the steps, an ungainly tangle of legs unravelling to let him get away down the lane. Susy had to be restrained, tackled like a forward. She boiled inside, her whole body vibrating with suppressed growls and unuttered barks. How lucky Brutus was to escape such fury, although he must have been eight times her weight and ten times her size!

We laughed at her. We were overjoyed to see her so full of life and high spirits. She played like a pup again. We knew there was only today. Living with Susy was again the delight of our lives and time had no meaning when she took us for walks, pushed to get a place she wanted in the car, bundled in front of me when I went to search for something in the potting shed, or stood for ages in the court on a cold moonlight night listening to small sounds my dulling hearing couldn't detect, for this was another of her little foibles. She wouldn't be hurried over anything. When she wanted to stand and sniff she shut off her hearing aid and became deaf to all entreaties. When she was enjoying the sounds and scents of the last hour she would let nothing spoil that enjoyment. 'Come on in, Sue!' I would command. She would stand like a small statue. 'You're getting wet!' I would tell her angrily, knowing that I would have to rub her down with a towel when she decided to come in. I knew she loved the fine rain. She also enjoyed being roughly towelled. When I had finished she would put first one jaw on the carpet and plough along it and then the other side of her face, drying her beard in sheer delight. She was back among the bushes as in the old days. She made her bed and barked for her supper, barked for a freshly-run bowl of water, dashed round the room to prove she was as good as new, like an old man taking a delight in showing that his operation had left him as good as ever he had been.

The vet had truly given Susy a second lease of life. She didn't know how old she was. We chose not to remember. We sometimes remarked that she didn't look her age. 'No one would believe that she is almost ninety,' we said, taking a liberty with even the most exaggerated figures of dog-to-human lifespan. No one would have believed Susy was as old as she was, or had come through the operation she had. She looked young for her age, a well-preserved little blond dog with only the slightest suggestion of stiff-ness in her back legs. She still bounced along the sheep tracks over the cliff. She still bored through bracken and gorse. Her appetite would have shamed a growing pup. Woe betide our family butcher when he sent the order without Susy's lambs' hearts!

20

The Old Dog

IT might be true to say that a dog, like a man, is as old as
it feels, but without knowing how a dog feels one judges by
its behaviour. There were times when Susy seemed to be
approaching her second childhood and I am quite sure
that dogs as well as men sometimes go through this phase
of rejecting the harshness of the adult world. How else
could we account for Susy's sudden bursts of mad romp-
ing and excited invitations to play with her. She would
spring to her feet and pick up a ball and try to play a game
with it, or gallop round to simulate hide-and-seek we had
played when she was a pup. She tired of the game much
sooner, for she galloped rather than ran, not because she
was so enthusiastic but because she wasn't quite so limber
as she had been. A gentle trot was all very well but she
couldn't race, and the nearest she could get to a fast canter
was breaking the trot to gallop. When she had enough she
would be short of breath. Like an old man she would
toddle off and settle to have a snooze. Anyone who per-
sisted in trying to get her back into the game would be
warned with a gentle and quite harmless growl that she
was no flighty, high-spirited young thing ready for anything, but a very old lady who could exert herself only so
much and needed her rest. We got used to her resting and
laughed when she snored. She dreamt of her puppyhood,

perhaps, or simply lived the game in sleep, for she would make small squeaking noises and her little old legs would sometimes jerk while the dream went on. When she was really exhausted she twitched more. She could snore and sometimes move and cover her nose with her paws as though she was aware of the unladylike noises she had been making.

Her daily ritual became more pronounced and I saw this as another characteristic of old age in humans. She would trot out in the morning and without dallying come trotting back again to jump into her bed. She would come at exactly the same time of day to growl and tell us that her stomach was feeling the pangs of hunger. I took her for a daily walk. We followed exactly the same route. She watched me to see when I was making preparations for the outing. We went whether it rained or shone. I would slip my feet into my boots, tie the laces and reach for my walking stick, and Susy would be there waiting to go. The excitement wasn't what it had once been, especially as the years crept up on both of us. She didn't seem to expect such wonderful discoveries in the bracken and gorse, but would pause and sniff with great concentration, almost absent-mindedness it seemed at times, and then go on. I seemed to hear her saying that she detected the game scent in the bramble clump. A cock pheasant had gone through, but not today, last night after we had passed. Here too, she had once started a rabbit that had gone bouncing away up to the foot of the cliff with nowhere to go there, against the sheer face, but back down again. How she had squealed and lost her voice barking after it! We walked at an old dog's pace. She sometimes looked back at me. Where was I? she might have been asking herself. What are we doing here? Old age had put that slightly blue tinge of failing sight on her eyes. She didn't hear so well and how her mind wandered when she wasn't quite up to scratch, for now she had other little complaints common to old age. She had a sort of dry eczema which was most persistent.

We took her to the vet and he diagnosed it as over-heating of the blood, a complaint with which many long-haired dogs are afflicted, even before old age. I had had some dealings with fox-hounds similarly plagued. They had been fed flaked maize, a high carbohydrate diet which quickly overheats the blood and causes a dog to scratch. Susy had never had very much starch in her diet, but now we struck out meal or dog biscuit of any kind. The drawback to this is that a dog needs something on which it can grind its teeth. Susy's teeth had never been too good. She was too old to have them out. The vet said it was more than she could stand, and infection of the gums could only be counteracted with more injections of antibiotic. Bad breath is another scourge of dogs in old age. Between injections for her itch which did good, and injections for her gums which brought temporary relief, Susy began to know the vet's surgery only too well. She didn't like needles, but even humans have been known to run away from these. Her eczema troubled her only in the heat of summer. She toddled on and made no complaint. In this a dog is a wonderful example to man. Acceptance of things we can't change is one of the secrets of living. If Susy couldn't run, she would walk. She still insisted on being out in front. Her walk invariably carried her at a faster pace than I could keep up. It was a tireless trot rather than a walk, but she never exerted herself to go so far ahead that she went out of sight. The walk up the lane would come to a standstill at the stile. A time had been when she was capable of jumping up from one flag step to the next and clearing the stile long before anyone could come up with her. In her old age she did her best, but almost invariably would slip back and have to wait to be lifted. Placed on one of the flags on the other side of the wall, she would plunge headfirst to the ground, recovering herself just in time and trundling on along the footpath. We would walk another hundred yards or so and turn up towards the cliff face, following a sheep track and then come downhill again, through the blackthorns along the outer side of our boundary wall and back to the stile. This little circuit we did day after day. In the end I would stop where we normally turned up towards the cliff and let the old dog wander on by herself. Sometimes she would look back for reassurance, and I would have to make one or two strides in her direction to mislead her into thinking I was following, and she would go on. Often she didn't even bother to look back but, lost in her own world of bushes and scents, complete the circuit without me. I would turn back along the footpath and stand at the stile waiting for her to come down through the blackthorns. She was sometimes so lost in her own affairs that she would stand for minutes on end staring into the distance and I would begin to wonder if the uphill grade might have been too much for her heart. One day, I felt, her heart would give out, and she would come to the end of the line. I hoped it would be this way. She of all creatures, deserved a quick and painless death. Just when I would be about to go up through the thorns to meet her, she would come down, stepping tenderly over the trailing stem of blackberry, avoiding the dogrose entanglement and looking at me with incomprehension. How had I managed to be there, in front of her, when she had been so sure I was walking behind? She never seemed to grasp the fact that I had retraced my steps to the stile. In her prime she would have known. The breeze would have carried my scent. She would have recognized my footsteps on the path, and would have come rushing down to greet me. Now she was baffled. It was all too much for her confused mind. She didn't object when I lifted her, carried her tenderly to the stile, climbed it with her in my arms, and put her gently down on the ground on the other side. She always understood we were on the last lap of her round trip and hurried from the stile down the footpath, between the blackthorns on one side and our wall and the wych elms on the other. She would wait for me at the gate without turning her head to see if I had arrived. This was another characteristic of old age, the patient, stoical waiting.

'Gently with Sue,' we would say to the family when they came home for a week-end.' Remember she's an old lady now.' It was hard for the children, growing to be men and women in their own right, to realize that Susy was an octogenarian at least. Susy would greet them with such delight that for a moment or two it seemed the warning was unjustified. She wasn't old. She would be a Peter Pan among dogs! Susy kept her end up. She played, but she rested. She seemed to know her limitations and would refuse to accompany me up the path to the little wood or along to the hens in the new orchard. Once she would have raced away ahead but now she jibbed and would desert me, even when I cajoled her and carried her up the steep slope. It was as though she couldn't bear the thought of trotting over stones—the hens had manufactured a scree from the slope above the path and the jumble of stones was painful to Susy when she walked over it. I would reproach her and Susy would drop her tail until it was almost between her legs and do her best to run back to the kitchen door. Did I not appreciate that she couldn't do things she used to do? I had to. She made it plain. We all have to recognize that life is not forever and a body begins to die almost from childhood.

How old is an old dog? It depends on the breed and the size. A working dog is quite old at ten or even eight years of age. Most large breeds have a comparatively short life. Like human giants, the wear and tear and the strain inflicted upon a large body is in ratio to bulk. Small dogs may live to be seventeen or eighteen years of age, if they are of reasonably natural breed and without the defects of inbreeding to achieve novel features—long bodies, long ears, etc. At fourteen Susy was promising to meet the vet's prediction that she would live to be a ripe old age. When we took her for her check-ups (she had never needed them in her prime, of course) she was pronounced as very good for her age. We were encouraged to think that Rory, from the same strain, was a year older and plodding on. We didn't think about her ultimate age, the date that might be put on a gravestone. We didn't think about death or gravestones.

A most extraordinary event was the reception Susy gave our two grandchildren when they arrived with their parents for a short holiday at the cottage. When the children had been small it had been Susy's habit to come to the bedroom and lie down and wait while a bedtime story was read. This had been an invariable part of her day. Whether she waited outside the bathroom at bath time or not, she never failed to show up in the bedroom for a session of Beatrix Potter or whatever book happened to be bedtime reading. She would lie with her head on her paws, apparently listening, if not to the adventures of Jemima Puddleduck at least to the sound of a much loved voice. When the grandchildren arrived they too, had their lively interlude in the bathroom followed by 'the story'. Susy not only seemed to love the little ones as much as she had loved the children with whom she had been brought up, but she lived it all again. She would be there in the bedroom, lying with her head on her paws, listening to Beatrix Potter's classics. She lingered on after all the goodnights had been said, the giggling and the drowsy conversations finally ceased, and all was quiet. When the children's day was over she would come lolloping down the steep stairs and come into the lounge like an adult. She surely must have felt that in some way she was in a familiar and happy world.

Although she spent much more time sleeping now, she liked to be noticed and be in vision, as the television cameramen have it. In a way she was, for she had discovered that when the television was on most people in the room looked at it. Where better to see them, and be seen, than to lie or sit immediately under the set? This was one of her favourite resting places. She would forgo the comfort of foam rubber and a soft pillow in her bed to be in our sight. She would sleep and wake up, look at us with half-closed eyes and go back to sleep again. When the set was switched off she would pop into her bed. If the bed happened to be rather near an overlarge fire she would amble round to the back of an armchair or settee and stretch out there until it was time for us all to retire. At bedtime I would pick up her bed and carry it with Susy sitting upright in it, up the stairs to our bedroom. In her old age she was winning all the way, established in the bedroom, as close to us as she could possibly get. She had striven for this from puppyhood. In old age people and dogs learn how to get their own way!

Now that she was old and having had her eccentricities as well as her infirmities advertised in *Country Life* Susy's welfare had become the concern of a great many people who read about her but it used to amuse me to think how completely oblivious she was to her fame. Another world might have been looking in on ours from outer space! How is Susy? readers would ask, and I would report on her condition once more. A lot of people were greatly pleased to learn she had reached her fifteenth birthday.

21

Susy's Last Day

SHE came downstairs on the last day of her life, bouncing
and bumping from step to step as she had done from
puppyhood. She stopped for a moment at her look-out
place between the stair rails and then went on. At the
kitchen door she waited for me to catch up with her and
open the door for her and waited again to be let out to the
court. This was her daily habit. She would carefully avoid
the metal grid at the doorstep because it tended to entrap
her small feet and she would pass round it to stand still for
a moment or two. I never really knew whether she was
simply collecting her wits or considering the day the way
an old person stands to weigh up the weather and make
comparisons with other mornings. At length she trundled
off up the path by the potting shed. I remember everything so well because we had been watching her very closely
for days past. About a fortnight before this she had had a
reccurrence of the gum infection that had plagued her so
much that we had begun to take her to the vet once a
month. The last injection seemed to have done a lot of
good but I had begun to wonder if she was really fit to
stand such heavy doses of antibiotic. There was something about her I couldn't quite place. Her reaction to
things wasn't the same. If anything she seemed livelier. It
was too good to be true, I felt, especially in a dog toddling
towards her sixteenth anniversary.

We had come to live with infirmity by this time, and could hardly let her out of our sight. Every dog, and especially when it gets old, needs privacy. We were unhealthily concerned if she slept too well. I had got into the habit of sitting up and listening for her breathing. I had a morbid fear that I would come upon her dead in her sleep, but this at least would have been peaceful and merciful. A quiet end is a blessing so few creatures know. Dogs die mangled by cars, crippled by rheumatism, dragged down by growths until their gaunt bodies and sad eyes compel their masters to have them put to sleep. For a long time we had discussed what should be done in the event of Susy's life seeming to be unrelievably miserable. It was really a question of euthanasia. I felt that the decision was mine. The moment I recognized suffering beyond evidence of temporary pain or something a drug would alleviate I would have Susy put to sleep, I said. The awful dilemma lay in the fact that I loved the dog so much I would hesitate to decide that this moment had really arrived. I knew it, and I knew the time was at hand, tomorrow, or the day after perhaps.

Christmas was only a week away. We had planned to go south to spend a few days with the children. Our plans depended upon how Susy was. If she could manage the journey without discomfort, we said, the family would be delighted to see her. The grandchildren would make her think she was young again. It was a long way to go, however, a round trip of almost five hundred miles. We had arrangements to make, for we couldn't just get up and go with a company of hens and ducks to be provided with food and water and locked up at night. Susy looked game enough. She came in from her morning toddle and growled her usual greeting. I laughed when she ran in a circle and seemed to want to play. I was reassured, relieved. She would live forever—and then all at once she keeled over! I picked her up but she had recovered, even though the bright look was gone from her eye. I carried her to her bed and reported the alarming event to my wife. We stood looking at Susy sleeping in her blanket. I was sure she had had a heart attack, however short the attack had been. Such a thing had never happened to her before.

'I think she's coming to the end,' I said. I have always been unable to keep this kind of depressing thought to myself. The echo was no different. This day wasn't like any other day in the dog's life. She had been off her food, sick, listless, but she had never fallen off her feet as though switched off. The fact that she slept was no consolation now. If she slept she wouldn't exert herself but when she awoke she would want to move about and that might be enough to bring on another attack. To my surprise Susy awoke and trotted to the kitchen as though nothing had happened. Old people have 'turns' I told myself. Susy had had one. She might not have another for months. How foolish I always was, looking on the black side, glooming about things that were far off and might never happen! She would be all right. She would be with us for years. We would take her to London and she would sit up watching the passing scene as I drove down there.

'She'll be fine. She's all right!' we repeated over and over again. Susy wagged her tail and looked up at us with an expression that seemed to be intended to tell us that we were not to worry. She knew what it was all about. Anthropomorphism is incurable I am inclined to think, but it comes in spasms. We read what we want to read into animal behaviour. It is hard to believe that a dog stands with nothing in its head when its reactions so plainly indicate that it is very much affected by human emotions. It is distressed when people quarrel, it is delighted when they play. It is cast down when they are in misery. Susy's apparent recovery was misleading because a dog doesn't dwell on what has gone before. Its reactions have been conditioned by its having done things which resulted in pain, but pain such as a heart attack would have no association with anything external. Susy carried on. It was gone, over and done with, leaving no mark. Our relief was childish. We had visitors coming to tea that day, old friends who had the same feeling for animals as we had ourselves. Susy welcomed them as she welcomed everyone, and came ambling into the lounge to enjoy the fire and perhaps a small corner of a sweet biscuit if anyone felt inclined to offer it. Our friends remarked on her liveliness and her brightness considering her age.' Yes,' we said, 'She will be sixteen in May.'

After a little while Susy led me to the door. She wanted to go out. I opened it for her and she walked a few paces and stood still for a long time before going on. I watched her go and then something made me change into my shoes and follow. I had a feeling that she was walking away to die. She walked onto the rosebed and straight on through it until she came to the brink of the path on the far side. Before I could do anything about it she went over the edge and fell on her side, whimpering. I rushed round and picked her up. I knew now, without the slightest doubt, that this was her last day. She had come to the end. My wife had hurried out to see what was wrong. We went back indoors and put Susy in her bed while I telephoned the vet. A heart attack, I said, the second that day. I felt guilty that I hadn't made the call in the morning, knowing that I had shirked it. The vet's wife told me to bring Susy to the surgery. Her husband was out, but he would 'see her' as soon as he got in.

'This is the end,' I said. 'She simply mustn't be allowed to suffer another attack! I should have taken her this morning.'

On many previous occasions when Susy had had injections my wife had taken the brunt of the ordeal, now I knew it was my turn. I would take her to be put to sleep and stand by while it was done. Our friends were very understanding and insisted upon taking their leave at once. We lifted Susy's bed with her in it and carried it out to the car. I felt as though I had swallowed a large stone.

The journey to the vet's surgery beyond the old town of Conwy passed so quickly that I was almost dazed to find we had arrived. I sat for a moment or two and then got out and picked up Susy and carried her in. The vet handled her very gently. 'I can hardly find a heart-beat,' he said. 'She's at the end, poor old thing.' There was nothing else to be done. I stood back while the vet and his assistant prepared the needle and gave her her last injection. She didn't twitch or quiver but seemed to be instantly asleep. I picked her up, choked on my words of thanks and blundered out through the door to the car. Tears blinded me. I put her back on her bed and sat still until I could see well enough to drive. Our mutual anguish was all that we could bear. I remember nothing of the journey home. When we reached the cottage I went inside and put on lights so that the court and the slope above could be illuminated for I knew what I had to do. I had to bury her and have done with the unbearable misery that was reducing me to nothing. I got a small spade from the potting shed and went up under the pines and dug her grave. When it was deep enough I came down and lifted her from the car and took her up and buried her, covering her with her blanket for some reason I can't really explain.

We did our best to console one another saying that she had lived a long time. She couldn't have survived, nor could I have allowed her to suffer another attack. I went to bed and couldn't sleep for thinking about her and the way she had changed my whole outlook, the way she had influenced our lives, the life of the family. How could a small dog do so much to people? How could people allow themselves to be so controlled by a small animal? Let the world say what they like about sentimentalists. What kind of creature is a man without sentimentality after all? So many people who disclaim sentimentality would be forced to admit that the completely cold individual is seriously deficient and something less than a low form of animal.

Susy wasn't dead, however. She haunted me. I stepped over her and walked round her. I heard her bark. I even saw her trundling down the path from the garden. More than once, thinking, or not thinking that she was there, I called to her to come on and chase a mouse in the potting shed. I stared out of the window waiting to see her come across the court. I couldn't believe that she was buried up there on the slope. She was asleep somewhere and she would appear as though nothing had happened. Everything was part of an awful nightmare. I wrote her obituary within a day of her death, not as a piece of journalism but an expression of my feelings. It was as objectively done as anything I had ever written. I could see myself from the outside. I had badly needed to be loved by my dog. I had, as the poet said, been God to her.

The advice of a great many people who wrote to me was to get another dog at once. I had no inclination to do anything of the kind. It seemed no one could understand this. It wasn't anything to do with my need to have a dog. On the other hand I might have sworn not to have another for purely selfish reasons, the thought that another dog might come to the same end before I met mine. There would never be another dog like Susy. To replace her with any kind of dog was out of the question. She was unique. She was in my memory, a thing I had loved as much as I could love anything.

A year afterwards I feel no different. I mourn her loss as acutely as ever with the difference that I remember the endless pleasure she gave me, the delight I took in everything she did. Whoever it was that said a man is blessed if he has known one good woman and had one good dog had a great assessment of happiness, a good yardstick to measure the quality of life.

We talk of her regularly, remembering the way she burrowed under the carpet, the way she danced on her hind legs for her liver and lambs' hearts, and her fury when some strange dog intruded upon her territory. She is revered like an old grandmother. There will never be another dog like her. There never could be, and there is nothing more to be said.

NON-FICTION BIOGRAPHY

GENERAL NON-FICTION

GENERAL NON-FICTION